CW00820886

the

lemon

cookbook

the *lemon* cookbook

50 Sweet & Savory Recipes *to* Brighten Every Meal

ELLEN JACKSON

Photography by John Valls

SASQUATCH BOOKS
SEATTLE

For my husband Steven,
who never makes me pucker
and always makes me smile

Copyright © 2015 by Ellen Jackson

All rights reserved. No portion of this book may be reproduced or
utilized in any form, or by any electronic, mechanical, or other means,
without the prior written permission of the publisher.

Printed in China

Published by Sasquatch Books

19 18 17 16 15   9 8 7 6 5 4 3 2 1

Editor: Susan Roxborough
Project editors: Michelle Hope Anderson and Em Gale
Photographs: John Valls
Design and Illustrations: Joyce Hwang
Food styling: Ellen Jackson
Copy editor: Diane Sepanski

Library of Congress Cataloging-in-Publication Data is available.

ISBN: 978-1-57061-982-3

Sasquatch Books
1904 Third Avenue, Suite 710
Seattle, WA 98101
(206) 467-4300
www.sasquatchbooks.com
custserv@sasquatchbooks.com

contents

recipe list

Sweets 69

Drinks 95

Staples 105

introduction

I was first seduced by a lemon at the tender age of six. A lemon stick, to be exact. A signature item of the annual FlowerMart in Baltimore, lemon sticks—a peppermint stick unceremoniously jammed into a lemon—are a staple of the city's springtime fairs and festivals. I drew the juice of my lemon up through the porous peppermint candy, smitten with the fruit's bitterness and the way it made my entire mouth pucker. I was in lemon love.

Lush-leaved lemon trees are as common as backyard swimming pools in California, where we moved when I was nine. Throughout the year, the air is perfumed with their scent, especially that of the thin-skinned, marigold-yellow Meyer lemon. There are rough-skinned, egg-shaped Eureka and Lisbon lemons too, in shades of pale yellow and green. But their sunny appearance belies what's inside—a fruit nearly impossible to eat, as the Peter, Paul and Mary song goes: "Lemon tree, very pretty, and the lemon flower is sweet, but the fruit of the poor lemon is impossible to eat."

A lemon's unapologetic acidity—sharp enough to create a honeycomb tunnel from one end of my peppermint stick to the other—imparts an intense freshness as vital to coaxing good flavor from your cooking as salt. A squirt of lemon juice brightens savory dishes and gives an unmistakable edge to desserts. Lemon zest adds a punch of lemony flavor to everything from rich goat cheese gnocchi (page 37) and creamy risotto (page 54), to cornmeal waffles (page 9) and beloved lemon bars (page 73). Whole lemons—preserved, pickled, pureed, salted—become delicious condiments, their sourness subdued by the similarly bold flavors of the Middle East and Southeast Asia. Strips of lemon peel garnish cocktails and infuse the contents of simmering pots with potent lemon essence. Though I am committed to cooking primarily with ingredients that grow close by and are in season, I'll make an exception for lemons without hesitation.

Lemons are always available, but you may have noticed that citrus is best in the winter months, when its presence in a rich dish is most dramatically transformative and balancing. The strong, clear flavor of lemons cuts through the heaviness of the fatty foods we indulge in during the holidays, and the best marmalade is made with winter fruit. But lemons have an insistent personality that allows them to play a leading yet complementary role throughout the year, when paired with more delicate ingredients such as spring vegetables, summer berries, and eggs and cream.

So what qualifies a dish for inclusion in a lemon cookbook? That was something I asked myself often when developing these recipes. Some contain entire lemons—peel, pulp, and pith—announcing proudly, "I am lemon, hear me roar." Others get plucky flavor from the fruit's zest and its essential oils. Still others are remarkably enhanced by a simple, judicious squeeze of lemon. Refreshing and versatile, lemons have a place in our drinks, on our pizzas, and at our breakfast tables. Zest and juice them, yes, but roast, grill, and preserve them too. And when spring comes around, pierce one with a peppermint stick; I guarantee it'll make you pucker—and smile.

a lemon primer

A lemon is a lemon is a lemon, right? Not exactly. For all their ubiquity and uniformity, a closer look reveals that lemons come in different varieties, shapes, and sizes. Some are small and juicy, while others have thick jackets that hide surprisingly tasteless, juiceless pulp. A lemon can be used from the inside out, each part bringing its own unique qualities to your cooking and baking. Read on for tips on choosing the best lemon, figuring out what it will yield, and getting the most from it.

Lemon Varieties

Nearly 95 percent of the lemons grown in the United States come from California and Arizona, with the balance from Florida. Although there are few opportunities for most of us to enjoy a truly local lemon, there's a source on either end of the country, and they're available year-round. The two main lemon varieties, Eureka and Lisbon, are nearly identical in appearance, large and egg shaped with finely pitted skin. The only way to tell them apart is the time of year: Eurekas are

Lemons Are Good for You

When it comes to natural health benefits, lemons lead the pack. They contain unique flavonoid compounds that have antioxidant and anti-cancer properties, and are valued for their antibiotic effects.

In addition to containing a multitude of phytonutrient benefits, lemons are a source of other essential nutrients including vitamin A, beta-carotene, calcium, magnesium, folate, phosphorous, and potassium, many of which are contained in its peel. They are especially rich in vitamin C, one of the most important antioxidants found in food. Vitamin C is essential for maintaining a fully functional immune system, aiding digestion, balancing the body's pH levels, fighting tumors, and helping wounds to heal more quickly.

a summer variety, and Lisbons are plentiful in the fall.

Meyer lemons are a cross between a lemon and an orange or tangerine. Floral and very aromatic, their juice is sweeter and should be used in combination with regular lemon juice if you're looking to add acidity to a recipe.

How to Choose a Lemon

Choosing a fresh, juicy lemon isn't about finding the one with the most vibrantly colored skin. Instead, look for fruit with an allover natural sheen, indicating that the lemon has retained its essential oil. The skin should be free of soft spots and excessive texture or pitting, and the fruit should be plump and feel heavy. Though you might guess that the weight is in the juice, it's actually in the sugar. Ripeness in citrus fruit is measured by sweetness, using the Brix/acid ratio, better known for measuring the sugar in wine grapes.

Because their skin is porous, lemons absorb whatever they've been sprayed with. For that reason alone, it's worth seeking out organic lemons. They tend to be thinner skinned and juicier than the larger conventional lemons, which are often dyed for even color and coated with wax. In my experience, grocery stores often carry two-pound bags containing eight organic lemons that rarely end up being more expensive than those for sale by the each.

If you can't find organic lemons, wash the fruit well in lightly soapy warm water with a soft vegetable brush.

It's All in the Zest

The skin of the lemon—commonly referred to as the zest—is the source of its potent flavor, while the juice contains the tart, acidic qualities not found in the fruit's jacket. Use zest if you want to infuse your food and cocktails with intense, bright lemon essence.

The key to removing the zest is to take the lemon's thin top yellow layer and leave as much of the bitter white pith behind as possible. Finely grated zest releases more of the fruit's volatile oil—hence flavor—than large strips, so choose your zesting tool according to the intensity of flavor your dish requires. Always zest into the bowl or pan you'll use in the course of making the recipe to catch the mist of lemon oil that's released as you remove the skin.

Tools for zesting

The shallow blades of a traditional *five-hole zester* remove thin strands from the top layer of the peel. The long strands can be used whole, to infuse an item with flavor, or chopped. When a recipe calls for finely or coarsely chopped zest, use a traditional zester to remove the peel. An average, or medium, 4- to 5-ounce lemon will yield 1 tablespoon of chopped zest.

Bartenders use a *channel knife* to make the curly twist of citrus traditional in cocktails. But it's the lemon oil that is released with the twist that adds the flavor.

Use a *vegetable peeler* with a Y-shaped handle and sharp blade to remove 1-inch-wide strips of peel for candying and infusions. One average, or medium, 4- to 5-ounce lemon will yield seven or eight strips of peel.

A *box grater* is one way to get finely grated zest. Stretch a piece of plastic wrap over the side of the grater with the smallest holes and, holding it taut, grate as usual. The zest (and precious essential oils) will end up on the plastic wrap rather than stuck in the holes of the grater and can be easily and thoroughly removed.

Grated this way, one average, or medium, 4- to 5-ounce lemon yields about 2 teaspoons of finely grated zest.

A *Microplane/rasp* can also be used for finely grated zest. Fast and easy to use, it gently removes the yellow skin (leaving the pith behind) and essential oils in a fine, feathery zest—just rub the fruit against it with quick downward strokes, rotating as you go, to get the zest all the way around. One average, or medium, 4- to 5-ounce lemon yields approximately 1 tablespoon of lightly packed, finely grated zest.

How to Juice a Lemon

If lemon is the flavor you're highlighting in a recipe (think lemon bars or curd), there's no substitute for fresh lemon juice. You've probably noticed the off-flavor that most bottled lemon juice has, more acidic than bright. That's because the bottled stuff usually contains additives such as sugar and water, as well as preservatives, including citric acid and sulfites. If it's acidity rather than lemon flavor you're after, try vinegar instead.

To keep plenty of fresh lemon juice on hand without worrying about a bag of lemons going bad, get out the juicer. First though, remove the zest, as it's more difficult to zest fruits after juicing. Store the zest in a small airtight plastic container in the freezer for up to six months. Add to your supply whenever you need lemon juice but not the zest. Next, juice the fruit and freeze it in small portions in something like an ice cube tray. When the cubes are frozen, pop them out into a zippered bag. The small amount defrosts quickly and can even be added directly to hot foods.

Tips for juicing

To get the most juice, start with a clean, dry lemon and use the palm of your hand to apply gentle pressure as you roll the fruit against the cutting board. Halve the fruit crosswise. (Though there's a school of thought that a lemon halved lengthwise yields more juice than one cut crosswise, that's not been my experience.) Room-temperature lemons will usually yield a bit more juice than cold ones.

Tools for juicing

A *reamer* (or fork) is a low-tech, inexpensive tool that is also one of the most effective for juicing. The idea with both the reamer and fork is to hold the cut fruit in one hand, plunge the tool in with the other, and twist it so that it grabs and presses the flesh of the fruit, releasing the juice. (This also releases the seeds, which is the only drawback.) There are reamer attachments for stand mixers too.

Hand juicers operate on the same principal as reamers, but they have a saucer to catch the seeds. Place the lemon half over the reamer cap and twist, using light pressure, to release the juice and little bits of the flesh.

A *handheld citrus press* cradles the citrus half in the concave side of the juicer, cut side down. When the convex dome is lowered onto the citrus, it flips it inside out, effectively removing all the juice and none of the seeds or pulp.

How much juice is in a lemon?

The amount of juice you'll extract from a lemon varies widely, based on the size of the fruit, its temperature (cold fruit yields less juice), and the method used to extract the juice. For the most part, the larger the lemon, the more juice it will give you; thick-skinned, conventionally grown lemons which can weigh up to one-half pound each are an exception to this rule.

One small organic lemon, weighing 3 to 4 ounces, contains around 2 tablespoons of juice, while an average, or medium, 4- to 5-ounce lemon will yield up to ¼ cup of juice. A conventional lemon weighing 7 to 8 ounces will yield about ¼ cup plus 1 tablespoon of juice.

How to Peel and Segment a Lemon

The best way to peel a lemon (and most other citrus) is to begin by slicing off enough of the blossom and stem ends to expose some of the pulp. Then stand the fruit on one of its flat sides on a cutting board. Using a small sharp knife, cut away the peel and white pith, following the natural curve of the fruit. When you are finished, the flesh will be completely exposed. Shave off any stray bits of pith. To remove the segments (also called supremes), work over a bowl to catch any juice as you cut the pulp away from the membranes connecting them, allowing the fruit segments to drop into the bowl with the juice.

How to Store Lemons

If kept away from direct sunlight, lemons will stay fresh at room temperature for about one week. Store them in the crisper drawer of the refrigerator for longer periods of time, up to about one month.

Using Nonreactive Cookware

Reactive cookware and equipment made from aluminum, cast iron, or copper can impart a metallic taste and/or cause discoloration in certain foods, especially acidic or alkaline ingredients like lemon juice, vinegar, and salt. When a recipe calls for a nonreactive bowl or pan, use glass, enamel, ceramic, or stainless steel to avoid such a reaction.

breakfasts

Baked Eggs with Lemon, Cream,
and Poppy Seeds *3*

David's Double-Lemon Dutch Baby *5*

Lemon Muffins with
Crystallized Ginger *7*

Lemon Cornmeal Ricotta Waffles *9*

baked eggs *with* lemon, cream, *and* poppy seeds

This combination was loosely inspired by a pasta dish on the menu at Emily, a restaurant in Brooklyn. Eggs and lemon get along famously, and I like the idea of pairing the two with poppy seeds in a savory dish. Using both lemon oil and zest provides a complex hit of flavor.

This simple dish deserves the best, freshest eggs you can find. Serve it with a crusty baguette, split down the middle and lightly toasted, for scooping and dipping. Add a small green salad and you have the makings of an elegant lunch or brunch. Note that you'll need to use 4½- to 5-inch ramekins for individual servings.

MAKES 4 SERVINGS

Preheat the oven to 350 degrees F.

Thoroughly coat the bottom and sides of 4 ovenproof ramekins or baking dishes, using 1½ teaspoons of the oil for each. Put the ramekins on a baking sheet with sides (to make moving them in and out of the oven easier).

Divide the shallot among the ramekins, adding no more than 2 teaspoons per dish. Add 1½ teaspoons of the zest and 1 tablespoon of the cheese to each ramekin, cover with 1 tablespoon of the cream, and season with a pinch of salt.

Carefully crack 2 eggs into each dish, starting with a new one if the yolk breaks. Pour 2 tablespoons of the remaining cream over each yolk and sprinkle it with 1 tablespoon of the remaining cheese, ½ teaspoon poppy seeds, and a pinch of salt. Bake for 10 to 12 minutes, or until the eggs are just slightly set. Garnish each egg with 1 teaspoon of the chives and serve immediately.

6 teaspoons Lemon-Infused Olive Oil (page 112), extra-virgin olive oil, or melted butter, divided

1 medium shallot, finely minced, divided

2 tablespoons finely grated lemon zest, divided

1 ounce Parmesan cheese, finely grated (about ½ cup), divided

¾ cup heavy cream, divided

Kosher salt

8 eggs, at room temperature

2 teaspoons poppy seeds, divided

4 teaspoons finely chopped fresh chives, divided

david's double-lemon dutch baby

This custardy, oven-baked pancake goes by several different names, but when I was growing up, we called it David Eyre's Pancake, which is what Craig Claiborne dubbed it in his 1966 *New York Times* column. The first time my mother made the pancake, my sister and I watched it swell and soufflé around the edges through the oven window, at least as excited about what it was doing as how it would taste. Somewhere along the way, because I love its flavor in baked goods, I started adding cardamom to the batter and rechristened the pancake David's Dutch Baby, a nod both to cardamom's wide use in Scandinavian cooking and its other, equally popular name. Be sure to buy cardamom encased in its pod and grind the seeds fresh for the best flavor. This is a favorite on Saturday mornings at my house.

MAKES ONE 10-INCH PANCAKE

Preheat the oven to 425 degrees F and place a rack in the middle of the oven.

In a small bowl, stir together the flour, granulated sugar, and salt. Finely grind the cardamom seeds using a mortar and pestle or clean coffee grinder and add to the dry ingredients. Set aside.

In a large bowl, lightly whisk the eggs with the milk and zest. Add the dry ingredients and lightly whisk until blended. The batter doesn't have to be completely smooth, but make sure there aren't any large lumps of flour.

continued

1 cup unbleached
   all-purpose flour

1 tablespoon granulated
   sugar

Generous pinch of
   kosher salt

Seeds from 4 to 5 green
   cardamom pods (about
   ¼ teaspoon seeds)

4 eggs

1 cup whole milk

1 tablespoon finely grated
   lemon zest

¼ cup (½ stick) unsalted
   butter

¼ cup confectioners' sugar

2 tablespoons freshly
   squeezed lemon juice

In a medium (10-inch) cast-iron skillet over medium-high heat, melt the butter, swirling the pan occasionally, until the butter is very hot and foamy, and almost beginning to brown. Immediately pour in the batter and put the skillet in the oven. Bake for 20 minutes, or until the edges are billowy and brown and the center of the pancake has puffed up. Remove the pan from the oven, sprinkle the pancake evenly with the confectioners' sugar, and return it to the oven for 2 to 3 more minutes. Sprinkle the lemon juice over the top and serve immediately.

lemon muffins *with* crystallized ginger

A whole lemon, finely chopped, and a small handful of crystallized ginger punch up the flavor of these muffins in the winter months. Come summer, swap the ginger for fresh blueberries or huckleberries for a lemony twist on a familiar breakfast favorite. If you're looking to impress, scoop the batter into tulip baking cups. Cooled, glazed, and garnished with candied lemon peel or crystallized ginger pieces, they could probably be passed off as dessert!

MAKES 1 DOZEN MUFFINS

Preheat the oven to 350 degrees F. Line a standard 12-cup muffin tin with paper liners or lightly butter and dust it with flour.

In a small bowl, whisk together the flour, baking powder, salt, and baking soda. Set aside.

Trim the blossom and stem ends of the lemon, removing enough rind that the pulp shows, then halve it. Gently squeeze each half over a bowl to loosen the seeds and remove some of the juice before cutting the halves into smaller pieces, removing any seeds as you go. Place the pieces and juice in a blender or the bowl of a food processor and process until the largest pieces are the size of a grain of rice. Set aside.

In the bowl of a stand mixer fitted with the paddle attachment or using a handheld electric mixer, beat the butter and sugar on medium-high speed until light and fluffy, about 5 minutes. Using a spatula, scrape the sides of the bowl, then reduce the speed to medium and add

1¾ cups unbleached all-purpose flour

2 teaspoons baking powder

¾ teaspoon kosher salt

½ teaspoon baking soda

1 small thin-skinned lemon

10 tablespoons (1¼ sticks) unsalted butter, at room temperature

1 cup sugar

2 eggs

1 teaspoon vanilla extract

1 cup whole milk Greek yogurt

½ cup plus 3 tablespoons coarsely chopped candied ginger, divided

FOR THE GLAZE:

½ cup confectioners' sugar

1 tablespoon plus 1 teaspoon freshly squeezed lemon juice

continued

the eggs one at a time, mixing until thoroughly combined. Add the vanilla and beat several seconds.

Add one-third of the dry ingredients and incorporate on low speed, then increase the speed to medium and mix for 1 minute. Add half of the yogurt and mix briefly to incorporate. Add half of the remaining dry ingredients and incorporate on low speed before increasing the speed to medium for 1 minute. Repeat with the remaining yogurt and dry ingredients. Using a spatula, scrape the bottom and sides of the bowl and fold in the chopped lemon and ½ cup of the candied ginger. Use an ice cream scoop to distribute the batter evenly among the prepared muffin cups.

Bake for 35 to 45 minutes, or until the muffins spring back to the touch. Transfer to a wire rack to cool completely before glazing.

To make the glaze, in a small bowl, mix the confectioners' sugar and lemon juice with a fork until smooth. Spoon a small amount on each muffin, spreading it slightly with the back of the spoon. Finely chop the remaining 3 tablespoons crystallized ginger and sprinkle it over the muffins.

lemon cornmeal ricotta waffles

This batter puffs up enthusiastically when it hits a hot griddle, so don't let the lack of a waffle maker get in the way of whipping up a batch. The thick batter takes longer to cook through than some pancake batters, so be sure to start with a hot pan over medium heat, adjusting the heat as you go. If you opt to slip in slices of banana or a handful of fresh blueberries, make sure you cook the pancakes an extra minute or two on each side.

I like to eat these topped with fresh fruit and powdered sugar, but I doubt you'd be unhappy if you went with warm maple syrup, homemade jam, or a drizzle of honey instead.

MAKES ABOUT 1 DOZEN 4-INCH BELGIAN WAFFLES, OR SIXTEEN 3-INCH PANCAKES

Preheat the oven to 200 degrees F. Preheat the waffle iron according to the manufacturer's instructions.

In a large bowl, stir together the flour, cornmeal, sugar, baking powder, salt, nutmeg, and baking soda. In a medium bowl, whisk the milk, lemon juice and zest, and eggs, then whisk in ¼ cup of the butter. Add the wet ingredients to the dry, mixing just until moistened. It's okay if some lumps remain. In a small bowl, break up any clumps of ricotta using a fork and mix in the vanilla. Gently fold the cheese into the batter using a spatula. Do not overmix; the batter may be thick and slightly lumpy.

continued

- 2 cups unbleached all-purpose flour
- ¼ cup cornmeal
- ¼ cup sugar
- 2 teaspoons baking powder
- 1 teaspoon kosher salt
- Scant ½ teaspoon freshly grated nutmeg
- ½ teaspoon baking soda
- 1 cup whole milk
- ⅓ cup freshly squeezed lemon juice (from 2 medium lemons)

Lightly coat the waffle iron with the remaining 2 table-spoons butter. Pour enough batter into the waffle iron to just cover the grid (about ⅓ cup). Close and cook per manufacturer's instructions until golden brown, about 2 to 3 minutes. Transfer cooked waffles to a baking sheet to keep warm while you make the rest.

If you're making pancakes, lightly coat a griddle with butter and melt the butter over medium heat. Working in batches, pour ¼ cup of batter per pancake onto the griddle. Cook until the surface is bubbling and the edges are slightly dry, about 4 minutes. Turn and cook until the bottom is golden brown, another 3 to 4 minutes. Transfer cooked pancakes to a baking sheet to keep warm.

2 tablespoons finely chopped lemon zest (from 2 medium lemons)

2 eggs

¼ cup (½ stick) plus 2 tablespoons unsalted butter, melted and cooled, divided

¾ cup Homemade Ricotta Cheese (page 108) or store-bought

1 teaspoon vanilla extract

Because reheated waffles taste every bit as good as those hot off the waffle iron, I usually put together and bake a full batch, even if the fresh ones are just for two. Let the extra waffles cool completely, put them in a ziplock freezer bag, and freeze for up to 2 months. For a spur of the moment breakfast treat, pop the frozen waffles (no need to thaw) into a toaster or toaster oven until hot and crisp. To reheat a larger batch, crisp them in a 350-degree F oven for about 10 minutes.

salads

Shaved Zucchini Salad with
Lemon and Marjoram *15*

Kale and Brussels Sprouts Salad with
Lemon–Brown Butter Vinaigrette *16*

Summer Tomato and Green Bean Salad
with Preserved Lemon Vinaigrette *19*

Cracked Wheat and Carrot Salad
with Preserved Lemon *20*

shaved zucchini salad with lemon and marjoram

Though you could also use mint or oregano, marjoram—oregano's soft-spoken little sister—pairs especially well with zucchini in this simple salad.

Salting the zucchini before assembling the salad causes it to wilt slightly and gives it enough flavor to stand up to the plucky lemon-forward dressing. Don't let it sit too long, however, or the zucchini will get squishy and wet, and lose any texture it once had. Long, thin shavings of Pecorino Romano or another salty sheep's milk cheese, made with a vegetable peeler, are a nice finishing touch.

MAKES 4 TO 6 SERVINGS

In a colander sitting over a bowl or in the sink, combine the zucchini ribbons and salt. Toss well to coat the ribbons and set aside for 10 minutes. After 10 minutes, gather up the zucchini in several large handfuls, and gently squeeze some of the moisture out of each.

In a large bowl, mix the lemon juice with the shallot and a small pinch of salt. Add the zest and whisk in the oil in a slow, steady stream. Stir in the marjoram and add the zucchini ribbons to the bowl, tossing to evenly coat them. Serve immediately, topped with the cheese shavings.

- 1½ pounds (about 3 to 4 small) zucchini, thinly sliced lengthwise on a mandolin or with a vegetable peeler
- 2 teaspoons kosher salt
- 3 tablespoons freshly squeezed lemon juice
- 1 small shallot, thinly sliced on a mandolin or finely minced
- 1 tablespoon finely grated lemon zest
- ¼ cup extra-virgin olive oil
- 1 tablespoon finely chopped fresh marjoram
- Pecorino Romano cheese shavings, for garnish (optional)

kale *and* brussels sprouts salad *with* lemon–brown butter vinaigrette

Think of this salad as a winter slaw, brightened with chunks of creamy avocado and nutty sunflower seeds. If you're so inclined, it's good with a little bit of citrus: sections of pink grapefruit, blood orange, or tangerine are all delicious additions.

MAKES 4 TO 6 SERVINGS

2 small bunches lacinato kale (about 1 pound), stems removed and leaves sliced into thin ribbons

8 ounces brussels sprouts (about 12 to 16), halved and thinly sliced

¼ small red onion, thinly sliced

½ cup (1 stick) unsalted butter, cut into small pieces

FOR THE VINAIGRETTE:

¼ cup white wine vinegar

⅓ cup freshly squeezed lemon juice (from 2 medium lemons)

1 tablespoon finely chopped lemon zest

2 tablespoons finely minced shallot

Pinch kosher salt

¼ cup extra-virgin olive oil

1 tablespoon honey

In a large bowl, combine the kale, brussels sprouts, and onion. Set the salad aside while you brown the butter.

In a small, light-colored pan that allows you to see the color of the butter, melt the butter over medium heat, swirling it occasionally to ensure it melts evenly. It will begin to foam and change color, from light yellow to golden brown to a slightly darker, toasty brown that smells nutty. Remove the pan from the heat and transfer the contents to a small heatproof bowl. The milk solids will have settled to the bottom of the pan and browned; leave as much of that sediment behind as possible. Set the butter aside.

In a medium nonreactive bowl, combine the vinegar and lemon juice with the zest, shallot, and a big pinch of salt. Whisk the oil into the warm butter and add the honey. Slowly drizzle the mixture into the vinegar and lemon juice, whisking constantly, until the vinaigrette emulsifies. Check the seasoning and add salt and pepper to taste.

Add about ¼ cup of the warm vinaigrette to the greens and massage them with your hands until they soften slightly and feel less raw. Continue to add the vinaigrette, a few tablespoons at a time, until the greens are well dressed but not soggy (reserve any extra vinaigrette for another use). Add the avocado and sunflower seeds, toss to combine, and serve immediately.

Freshly ground black pepper

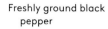

1 firm, ripe avocado, pitted and cubed

¼ cup toasted sunflower seeds

summer tomato *and* green bean salad *with* preserved lemon vinaigrette

This salad, simply dressed in a zippy, herbaceous vinaigrette, showcases the best of summer. Serve it with grilled fish, or skip the ricotta salata and add good-quality canned tuna and a few boiled potatoes for a quick Niçoise salad.

MAKES 8 SERVINGS

To make the vinaigrette, in a small, nonreactive bowl, combine the shallots and lemon juice with the salt. Set aside for 10 minutes to allow the shallots to soften and sweeten slightly. Then, add the mustard and honey, and slowly drizzle in the oil, whisking constantly, until the vinaigrette emulsifies. Stir in the herbs, lemon zest, and preserved lemon, and season to taste with salt and pepper.

In a medium bowl, toss the tomatoes with ½ cup vinaigrette and set aside to marinate for at least 20 minutes, or until you're ready to serve the salad.

While the tomatoes marinate, bring a pot of generously salted water to a boil. Cook the beans until they're just tender, about 4 minutes. Drain them in a colander and cool the beans by running them under cold water briefly. Spread them on a baking sheet lined with a clean towel. Set aside until completely cool and dry.

Just before serving, add the beans and ricotta salata shavings to the tomatoes and vinaigrette. Toss to combine the ingredients, add the remaining vinaigrette and season to taste with additional salt and pepper. Marinate for 10 minutes before serving.

FOR THE VINAIGRETTE:

1 tablespoon plus 1½ teaspoons finely minced shallot

3 tablespoons freshly squeezed lemon juice

Pinch kosher salt

1 tablespoon Dijon mustard

2 teaspoons honey

½ cup extra-virgin olive oil

6 tablespoons coarsely chopped soft herbs such as parsley, basil, tarragon, and chives

1½ teaspoons finely grated lemon zest

½ Preserved Lemon (page 107) or store-bought, flesh discarded and peel finely chopped

Freshly ground black pepper

. . . .

2 pints mixed cherry tomatoes, halved

1½ pounds green beans, trimmed

2 ounces ricotta salata cheese, shaved with a vegetable peeler

cracked wheat and carrot salad
with preserved lemon

There's a satisfying variety of flavors and textures at play in this recipe: salty, sweet, crunchy, and chewy from the cracked wheat. This is made by crushing raw wheat berries into smaller pieces in order to preserve the nutrient-rich bran and germ layers. If you're short on time, substitute bulgur, which is precooked, for the cracked wheat. Quinoa and millet are good gluten-free alternatives. All four ingredients can be found at well-stocked grocery and natural foods stores.

I don't rinse the preserved lemon; it usually has the right amount of salt to season the vinaigrette and salad. You may need to add more salt before serving, as the grains continue to absorb the flavors while the salad sits.

MAKES 4 TO 6 SERVINGS

1 cup cracked wheat

1 teaspoon kosher salt

½ Preserved Lemon (page 107) or store-bought

⅓ cup extra-virgin olive oil

2 to 3 tablespoons freshly squeezed lemon juice (depending on how lemony you like your dressing)

2 teaspoons coarsely chopped garlic

¾ teaspoon cumin seeds, toasted and ground

3 carrots, thinly sliced (about 2 cups)

In a heavy pan with a tight-fitting lid, place the cracked wheat and salt with 2 cups of water. Bring the water to a boil and reduce the heat to a simmer. Cover and continue to cook over the lowest heat, stirring occasionally, until the wheat is tender yet pleasantly chewy, 20 to 25 minutes. Drain any water that remains.

While the wheat is cooking, separate the pulp of the preserved lemon from the peel, remove the seeds, and add the pulp to a blender. Finely mince the peel and reserve it. Add the oil, lemon juice, garlic, and cumin seeds and blend until smooth.

Put the cracked wheat in a large bowl with the carrots, currants, and scallions, to allow the warm grains to soften the other ingredients slightly. Add half of the vinaigrette and the reserved lemon peel. Stir well to incorporate the vinaigrette. Taste the salad, adding more vinaigrette if it isn't flavorful enough. Let the salad sit for 15 minutes, taste again, and add pepper to taste and more vinaigrette if needed (reserve extra dressing for another use). Add the parsley just before serving.

⅓ cup currants

3 scallions, white and light green parts, thinly sliced

Freshly ground black pepper

1 cup lightly packed coarsely chopped flat-leaf parsley

sides

Toasted Cauliflower "Couscous"
with Lemon, Parsley, and Almonds *25*

Buttery Hedgehog Potatoes
with Lemon and Herbs *26*

Grilled Corn on the Cob with
Smoked Paprika-Lemon Butter *28*

Peppery Lemon
Parmesan Biscotti *30*

Lemon Miso-Roasted
Delicata Squash *32*

toasted cauliflower "couscous" with *lemon, parsley,* and almonds

Cauliflower has an uncanny ability to trick the mouth into believing it's consuming something laden with gluten or carbs, such as potatoes, rice, or, in this case, couscous. Whether it's finely chopped or pureed, the vegetable takes on buttery, silky qualities that don't show up when it's steamed or roasted.

MAKES 4 SERVINGS

Using a food processor with either the grating attachment or blade, grate or pulse the cauliflower in batches until it resembles grains of couscous. You should have about 4 cups. (You can also use a knife to dice the florets, which will easily break into very small pieces as you go.)

In a large, wide skillet over medium heat, toast the almonds, stirring frequently, until they smell nutty and are golden brown, about 7 minutes. Set the nuts aside and wipe out the pan. Warm 3 tablespoons of the oil over medium-high heat. When the oil is hot, add the cauliflower and salt. Sauté, stirring frequently, until the cauliflower pieces are toasted and tender, 12 to 15 minutes.

Remove the pan from the heat and immediately add the garlic and zest, stirring well to distribute the flavors throughout. After the mixture has cooled slightly, add the remaining 2 tablespoons oil, the lemon juice, almonds, and parsley. Season with additional salt and pepper, and allow the cauliflower to sit for at least 15 minutes, partially covered, for the flavors to develop. It is excellent at room temperature or can be rewarmed briefly over medium-high heat before serving.

1 (2-pound) head cauliflower, cut into small florets with ½-inch or less of stem

⅓ cup slivered almonds or pine nuts

5 tablespoons extra-virgin olive oil, divided

1½ teaspoons kosher salt

1 small garlic clove, finely grated or minced

1 tablespoon finely grated lemon zest

3 tablespoons freshly squeezed lemon juice

1 cup lightly packed flat-leaf parsley leaves, coarsely chopped

Freshly ground black pepper

buttery hedgehog potatoes
with *lemon* and *herbs*

Traditionally known as Hasselback potatoes, this dish is named for the Swedish restaurant where it originated, Hasselbacken. Hedgehogs, as I like to call this dish, are good with almost any potato, though I'm especially fond of Yukon Golds and Red Bliss potatoes. Repeated basting with olive oil and a plucky lemon-and-herb compound butter that dribbles down into the accordion folds has the effect of creating crispy edges surrounding a creamy, flavorful interior. A squeeze of lemon on the still-warm potatoes adds just the right hint of acidity.

MAKES 6 TO 8 SERVINGS

½ cup (1 stick) unsalted butter, at room temperature

3 tablespoons finely chopped fresh parsley

1½ tablespoons finely grated lemon zest (from 2 small lemons)

1 tablespoon finely chopped fresh marjoram

1 tablespoon finely chopped fresh chives

2 small cloves garlic

1 teaspoon kosher salt

2 tablespoons freshly squeezed lemon juice

In a small bowl, combine the butter with the parsley, lemon zest, marjoram, and chives.

Coarsely chop the garlic and sprinkle the salt over it. Continue to chop the garlic with the salt, holding the knife at a 30-degree angle to the cutting board and pulling it across the pile of garlic and salt to make a paste. Add the garlic paste and lemon juice to the butter and use a fork or the back of a spoon to incorporate it. Transfer the butter to a piece of plastic wrap and shape it into a log 1 inch in diameter. Refrigerate until firm, about 30 minutes.

Preheat the oven to 425 degrees F.

Using a wooden spoon to cradle the potato, slice the potatoes crosswise, making a cut every ¼ inch. (The spoon will prevent you from slicing all the way through and separating the slices from one another.)

Place the potatoes in a baking pan and brush them all over with the oil. Sprinkle them lightly with salt and pepper and bake for 30 minutes, or until the slices have begun to fan out slightly and separate from one another. Remove the pan from the oven and use a paring knife to nudge apart any slices that are sticking to one another. Place a small coin—or 2, depending on the size of your potatoes—of butter on top of each potato, pressing down gently to encourage it to melt down between the slices; you'll have some butter left over. Bake the potatoes for another 30 minutes, basting them occasionally with the butter in the bottom of the pan. They are done when the tops are slightly brown and crispy, and the middles are tender when pierced with a paring knife. Squeeze the lemon half over the potatoes and serve immediately.

20 egg-size Yukon Gold or Red Bliss potatoes (about 4 pounds)

2 tablespoons Lemon-Infused Olive Oil (page 112) or extra-virgin olive oil

Freshly ground black pepper

½ lemon

grilled corn on the cob with smoked paprika-lemon butter

When sweet corn is in season, there's nothing I'd rather eat for dinner than sliced tomatoes and two ears grilled like this. It tastes a little bit like the grilled corn sold by street vendors in Mexico that is slathered in garlicky mayonnaise and sprinkled with lime juice and crumbly Cotija cheese. Instead of mayonnaise, I baste the corn with a brown butter spread seasoned with plenty of lemon zest and juice, plus garlic, salt, and smoked paprika.

MAKES 6 SERVINGS

½ cup (1 stick) unsalted butter

1 tablespoon finely grated lemon zest

1 clove garlic, finely grated

3 tablespoons freshly squeezed lemon juice

½ teaspoon smoked paprika

1½ teaspoons kosher salt

6 ears fresh sweet corn

3 tablespoons coarsely chopped fresh cilantro

In a small, light-colored pan that allows you to see the color of the butter, melt the butter over medium heat, swirling it occasionally to ensure it melts evenly. It will begin to foam and change color, from light yellow to golden brown to a slightly darker, toasty brown that smells nutty. Remove the pan from the heat and transfer the contents to a small heatproof bowl. The milk solids will have settled to the bottom of the pan and browned; leave as much of that sediment behind as possible. Add the zest and garlic to the warm brown butter. Allow the butter to cool completely, then stir in the lemon juice, paprika, and salt.

Peel and discard the outer corn husks. Carefully pull back the pale-green inner husks and remove the silk. Cover the kernels with the husk again, tie the end with kitchen string, and soak the ears in cold water for at least 30 minutes.

Preheat a gas grill for high heat, about 450 degrees F, or prepare a charcoal grill for direct-heat cooking over red-hot coals. Remove the corn from the water, and shake off any excess moisture. Put the corn on the grill and close the lid. Turn the corn every 5 minutes, so that it cooks evenly, for 10 to 15 minutes. Untie the string, peel back the husks, brush the corn with the butter, and continue to cook with the husks peeled back until the kernels are caramelized on all sides, 3 to 5 more minutes.

Remove the corn from the grill, brush all over with more butter, and sprinkle with more salt to taste and the cilantro.

peppery lemon parmesan biscotti

These savory biscotti have it all: richness and umami from the cheese, brightness from the lemon, and a crunchy kick from the semolina and a generous dose of freshly ground black pepper. Serve them with wine, for dunking in soup, or with fruit and cheese.

MAKES ABOUT 3 DOZEN BISCOTTI

1½ cups unbleached all-purpose flour

½ cup semolina flour

2 ounces Parmigiano-Reggiano cheese, finely grated (about 1 cup)

2 tablespoons finely chopped lemon zest (from 2 medium lemons)

1 tablespoon freshly ground black pepper

2 teaspoons kosher salt

1 teaspoon baking powder

¼ cup extra-virgin olive oil

3 eggs, divided

⅓ cup whole milk

Preheat the oven to 350 degrees F.

In a large bowl, thoroughly combine the flours, cheese, zest, pepper, salt, and baking powder. Drizzle the oil over the top and use your fingers to gently incorporate it into the flour, until the mixture resembles cornmeal.

In a small bowl, whisk 2 of the eggs with the milk and add them to the flour mixture, stirring with a fork to form a soft, sticky dough. Lightly moisten your hands (to prevent the dough from sticking to them) and divide the dough in half. Arrange the pieces lengthwise on a baking sheet lined with parchment paper. Shape each piece into a log approximately 12 inches long, 3 inches wide, and ½ inch high, lightly wetting your hands as necessary to prevent sticking. Whisk the remaining egg and brush the logs with it.

Bake for 30 minutes, rotating the pan halfway through, or until the logs are pale golden brown. Remove the sheet to a rack and reduce the oven temperature to 300 degrees F. Cool the logs for 10 minutes, transfer them to a cutting board, and, using a serrated knife, cut each log diagonally into ½-inch-thick slices. Return the biscotti to the baking sheet and bake for another 35 to 45 minutes, turning them over halfway through the baking time. The biscotti are ready when they're dry and light golden brown on both sides. They will keep up to 2 weeks in an airtight container.

lemon miso-roasted delicata squash

One of my favorite things about delicata squash is its tender, entirely edible skin, which makes it the most user-friendly winter squash. These flavors are fabulous with carrots too, or try substituting cilantro for the parsley. You'll find white miso, made from soybeans that have been fermented with rice, in well-stocked groceries, natural foods stores, and Asian markets.

MAKES 4 TO 6 SERVINGS

3 tablespoons white miso

3 tablespoons extra-virgin olive oil

3 tablespoons freshly squeezed lemon juice, divided

1 tablespoon honey

2 teaspoons harissa

1½ pounds delicata squash (about 3 to 4), halved lengthwise, seeded, and cut into ½-inch thick moons

1 tablespoon finely grated lemon zest

½ cup coarsely chopped flat-leaf parsley

Kosher salt

Preheat the oven to 425 degrees F.

In a large bowl, whisk together the miso, oil, 2 tablespoons of the lemon juice, the honey, and harissa. Add the squash pieces to the bowl and use your hands to toss them with the paste, making sure to coat them evenly. Arrange them in a single layer on a lightly oiled baking sheet with sides. Set the bowl aside for later.

Roast the squash for 15 minutes. Remove the pan from the oven and, using tongs, turn the pieces over. Return them to the oven for 10 more minutes, or until the pieces are lightly caramelized and tender. Transfer the squash back to the bowl and toss with the remaining 1 tablespoon lemon juice, the zest, and parsley. Season to taste with salt.

vegetarian

Lemon–Goat Cheese Gnocchi with
Shelling Peas and Green Garlic *37*

Lentil-Chard Soup with
Lemon, Feta, and Dill *39*

Asparagus and Lemon Pesto Pizza
with Smoked Mozzarella *41*

Spaghetti with Radicchio, Ricotta,
and Lemon-Garlic Bread Crumbs *43*

Lemon Dal with Spinach and Yogurt *46*

lemon–goat cheese gnocchi *with* shelling peas *and* green garlic

The colors and flavors of this dish are the very essence of spring, but don't wait for daffodils to make an appearance before trying it. The rich, lemony gnocchi come together quickly, can be cooked ahead and refrigerated overnight, and pair equally well with flash-sautéed cherry tomatoes, shallots, and herbs in the summer; chanterelles and corn in the fall; and braised lamb or beef in the winter.

MAKES 6 TO 8 SERVINGS

In a large bowl, combine the cheeses, zest, salt, and eggs. Mix with a rubber spatula until smooth and add ¾ cup of the flour. Combine well and gently mix in the remaining flour to form a moist, slightly sticky dough. Do not over-mix or your gnocchi will be heavy. Cover the bowl with plastic wrap and refrigerate for 1 hour.

Lightly flour a baking sheet or large platter and set aside. Turn the dough onto a lightly floured work surface, form it into a ball, and cut the ball into quarters. Roll each quarter into a ½-inch-thick rope. Use a sharp knife to cut the ropes into ½-inch gnocchi and put them on the baking sheet. Repeat the process with the remaining dough pieces; you should get about 84. Lightly dust the gnocchi with flour. Bring a large pot of generously salted water to a boil.

continued

8 ounces slightly soft, mild fresh goat cheese, at room temperature

8 ounces cream cheese (preferably without stabilizers), at room temperature

1 tablespoon plus 1 teaspoon finely grated lemon zest (from 2 small lemons)

2 teaspoons kosher salt

2 eggs

1½ cups unbleached all-purpose flour, plus additional for rolling the dough

2 tablespoons extra-virgin olive oil

2 small stalks green garlic, thinly sliced on the diagonal, or 3 cloves garlic, finely chopped

¼ cup dry white wine or vermouth

3 cups freshly shelled
    green peas

3 tablespoons unsalted
    butter

2 tablespoons freshly
    squeezed lemon juice

1 tablespoon finely
    chopped fresh tarragon

Freshly ground black
    pepper

2 tablespoons fresh chives,
    cut into ½-inch lengths

Boil the gnocchi in batches of 15 to 20; they will take about 3 minutes to cook. They're done when they float—wait a few seconds before using a slotted spoon to remove the gnocchi to a baking sheet to cool. (They will be delicate when warm but will become sturdier as they cool.) Reserve 1 cup of the cooking liquid. The cooked gnocchi will keep in the refrigerator for 24 hours.

In a large skillet over medium heat, warm the oil. Add the garlic and cook, stirring constantly, until softened, about 4 minutes. Add the wine and simmer until the liquid in the skillet has reduced by half, 3 to 4 minutes.

Add the gnocchi, peas, butter, and ½ cup of the reserved gnocchi cooking liquid to the skillet. Cook until the ingredients are warmed through and the sauce thickens slightly, about 3 minutes. Add the lemon juice, tarragon, and salt and pepper to taste and toss to combine. Divide the gnocchi between 6 or 8 bowls. Garnish with the chives and serve immediately.

lentil-chard soup with lemon, feta, and dill

Earthy lentils are savored around the world, in part because they're complemented by everything from bacon and sausage to Indian spices to tart ingredients such as sorrel and lemon. Here they get a Greek twist, in the form of a spoonful of creamy feta cheese spiked with lemon and dill added to each bowl of soup before serving. Smear it on flatbread or toss it with pasta—this versatile and vibrant spread will inspire you to find new ways to use it. I like sheep's milk feta, which is creamier and less salty than other varieties.

MAKES 4 TO 6 SERVINGS

Halve the leeks lengthwise, cut them crosswise into ½-inch-thick slices, and wash them well in a colander. In a large stockpot or Dutch oven over medium-high heat, warm the oil. Add the leeks, shallot, and celery, and sauté until softened and translucent, about 7 minutes. Add the bay leaves and lentils, stirring to combine and coat with oil. Add the vegetable broth and salt and bring to a boil, over medium-high heat. Lower the heat and simmer, partially covered, until the lentils are nearly tender, 20 to 30 minutes.

Meanwhile, make the topping. Put the feta cheese in the bowl of a food processor with the lemon juice, zest, and garlic. Pulse several times to break up the cheese and slowly add the oil with the motor running. When the mixture is smooth, add the dill and pulse to coarsely

continued

8 ounces leeks, white parts and 1 inch pale green

2 tablespoons extra-virgin olive oil

1 large shallot, thinly sliced

2 stalks celery, thinly sliced

2 bay leaves

1½ cups French green or brown lentils, sorted and rinsed

6 cups vegetable broth or water

1 teaspoon kosher salt

FOR THE FETA TOPPING:

6 ounces feta cheese, preferably sheep's milk

2 tablespoons freshly squeezed lemon juice

1 tablespoon coarsely chopped lemon zest

1 small clove garlic,
coarsely chopped

¼ cup extra-virgin olive oil

¼ cup lightly packed fresh
dill sprigs

. . . .

2 tablespoons freshly
squeezed lemon juice

1 small bunch Swiss chard,
stems reserved for
another use and leaves
cut into 1-inch-thick
ribbons

Freshly ground black
pepper

Dill sprigs, for garnish

chop and incorporate it. Taste for seasoning, adding
more lemon juice if the cheese is particularly salty.

To finish the soup, stir in the lemon juice and chard ribbons and continue to simmer until the lentils are completely tender and the chard has wilted, 10 to 15 minutes.
Season to taste with salt, pepper, and more lemon juice
if desired. To serve, divide the soup among bowls, add a
spoonful of the feta topping, and top with a dill sprig.

asparagus *and* lemon pesto pizza *with* smoked mozzarella

A super-hot oven is the key to homemade pizza with a crispy crust. Begin pre-heating your oven while making the pesto to get it as hot as it should be.

Raw asparagus and a lemon half with its peel combine to create this fresh-tasting, chunky pesto. Look for fat asparagus spears for added textural interest and to minimize the chance of overpureeing them. Smoked mozzarella accents the "green" flavor of the pesto nicely, but regular fresh mozzarella is good too. The pesto is also excellent tossed with pasta or rice.

MAKES ONE 12- TO 14-INCH PIZZA

Position a rack in the center of the oven, place a pizza stone on it, and preheat the oven to 475 degrees F. (Use an inverted baking sheet if you don't have a pizza stone.) Dust a peel or a flat baking sheet (without sides) with cornmeal and set aside.

To make the pesto, in the bowl of a food processor, finely chop the lemon and garlic. Add the asparagus pieces (reserving the tips) and pistachios, pulsing until coarsely chopped. Add ⅓ cup of the oil all at once and process until the mixture is well combined but not pureed; it should look as if you've grated the asparagus, with pieces ranging in size from a grain of rice to grated cheese. Pour the mixture into a large bowl and add the cheese, salt, and pepper. Taste and add additional seasoning if necessary and set the pesto aside.

Cornmeal, for dusting

FOR THE PESTO:

½ lemon, seeded and cut into small pieces

2 small cloves garlic

1 pound asparagus, trimmed and cut into 1½-inch pieces, tips halved lengthwise

¼ cup toasted pistachios

⅓ cup plus 1 tablespoon extra-virgin olive oil, divided

2 ounces Parmigiano-Reggiano cheese, coarsely grated (about ½ cup)

1½ teaspoons kosher salt

continued

½ teaspoon freshly ground
   black pepper

. . . .

14 ounces homemade
   or store-bought pizza
   dough, at room
   temperature

6 ounces fresh smoked
   mozzarella cheese,
   grated or thinly sliced

On a lightly floured surface, roll out or stretch the pizza dough to make a 12- to 14-inch round and transfer to the prepared peel. (You can also form the round on a sheet of parchment paper and transfer it directly onto the pizza stone to bake.) Stir the pesto well, evenly spread about 1 cup over the dough, and arrange the mozzarella so that most of the pesto is covered. Toss the reserved asparagus tips with the remaining oil and scatter over the cheese.

Bake for 16 to 18 minutes, until the crust is deep brown and crispy and the asparagus pieces on top are lightly charred. (If you used parchment paper, bake for 8 to 10 minutes, pull the paper out from under the pizza so that the crust can crisp, and bake for 8 more minutes.) Remove the pizza from the oven and cool on a rack or baking sheet for 5 minutes before slicing.

The most important rule of homemade pizza? Less is more. Use a light hand when adding toppings to your crust, especially if the sauce that sits directly on top is slightly juicy, like tomato sauce or this pesto. Spread a super-thin layer on the dough, add the rest of the toppings, and finish with a few dollops of the saucy component scattered across the top for additional flavor.

spaghetti *with* radicchio, ricotta, *and* lemon-garlic bread crumbs

There are many good reasons to make and keep fresh ricotta on hand, but this pasta is one of the best. It hits most of the flavor receptors—bright, bitter, salty—and adds a creamy and crunchy texture to boot. Do not skip the bread crumbs. Lemony, garlicky, and slightly salty, they elevate this dish from pleasurable to memorable.

MAKES 4 TO 6 SERVINGS

In a large sauté pan over medium heat, warm ¼ cup of the oil. Add the garlic and cook, stirring occasionally, for 2 to 3 minutes, or until fragrant. Add the bread crumbs and a generous pinch of salt, and continue to stir until the bread crumbs are toasted and brown. Transfer the crumbs to a bowl and set aside to cool slightly. When they are cool, add the parsley and add 1 tablespoon of the zest. Season to taste with additional salt and pepper, and set aside.

Wipe any crumbs out of the pan, add the butter, and melt it over medium heat. When the butter is foamy, add the radicchio and cook until it wilts and softens slightly, 2 to 3 minutes. Add 2 tablespoons of water and simmer for 2 minutes, or until the water evaporates, then add 1 tablespoon of the lemon juice. Set aside.

continued

¼ cup plus 2 tablespoons extra-virgin olive oil, divided

4 cloves garlic, finely chopped

2 cups fresh bread crumbs

Pinch kosher salt

1 cup lightly packed, coarsely chopped flat-leaf parsley leaves

2 tablespoons finely chopped lemon zest (from 2 medium lemons), divided

Freshly ground black pepper

2 tablespoons unsalted butter

Bring a pot of generously salted water to a boil and cook the linguine according to the package directions. While it cooks, combine the ricotta with the remaining 2 tablespoons oil, 1 tablespoon zest, and 1 tablespoon lemon juice. Taste and add more juice if necessary. Before draining the pasta, set aside 1 cup of the cooking water.

Return the pasta to the pot. Add some of the pasta water to the ricotta mixture, to loosen it and warm it up, before tossing it with the pasta. Add the radicchio and half of the bread crumbs, and toss to combine, adding more of the pasta water if it appears dry. Place the pasta on a large platter and garnish with the rest of the bread crumbs. Serve immediately.

1 (1-pound) head radicchio, finely shredded

2 tablespoons freshly squeezed lemon juice, divided

1 pound good-quality spaghetti or linguine

1 cup Homemade Ricotta Cheese (page 108) or store-bought

lemon dal *with* spinach *and* yogurt

In Indian cooking, any and all varieties of dal, a dish of pureed legumes, can be flavored with *tadka*, a perfumed butter made by frying different combinations (dictated by region) of fragrant spices and seasonings, onions, ginger, garlic, and chiles in ghee, or clarified butter. Though it's not traditional, I like to imbue coconut oil with these flavors. The last-minute addition of lemon zest and juice seems to punch up each of the individual flavors, creating a whole that is more complex and memorable than the sum of its parts. Serve this dal with hot basmati rice.

MAKES 6 TO 8 SERVINGS

2 cups yellow split peas (*chana* dal), sorted and rinsed

1 teaspoon turmeric

1 small dried red chile, or 1 teaspoon red pepper flakes

¼ cup coconut oil or ghee, divided

1 tablespoon kosher salt

2 tablespoons unsalted butter

1 tablespoon brown mustard seeds

1 tablespoon coriander seeds, crushed

2 teaspoons cumin seeds

1 medium onion, cut into ½-inch dice (about 1½ cups)

In a large pot or Dutch oven, combine the peas, 6 cups of water, the turmeric, the chile, 2 tablespoons of the oil, and the salt. Bring the mixture to a boil, stirring occasionally to prevent the dal from sticking to the bottom of the pot. Lower the heat and simmer, partially covered, until the peas are very soft and tender, about 1 hour.

Meanwhile, make the *tadka*. In a large sauté pan over medium heat, warm the remaining 2 tablespoons oil and the butter. When the butter is foamy, add the mustard, coriander, and cumin seeds, stirring constantly until they are fragrant, about 2 minutes. Add the onion, increase the heat to high, and continue to cook until the onion goes from translucent to brown around the edges. This should take about 15 minutes; don't be afraid to get the onions dark. Add the cilantro and spinach, and continue to cook for about 5 more minutes, until both have wilted slightly but retain their bright color.

Remove the whole chile and stir the *tadka* into the peas. Season to taste with additional salt and cook over medium-low heat for 10 to 15 minutes to allow the flavors to combine. Add the lemon juice and zest and cook for another 5 minutes before serving. Garnish each portion with a spoonful of yogurt and a few cilantro leaves.

1 cup lightly packed, coarsely chopped fresh cilantro leaves, including some stems, plus additional leaves for garnish

2 cups lightly packed fresh spinach leaves

¼ cup freshly squeezed lemon juice (from 1 medium lemon)

2 teaspoons finely grated lemon zest

Whole milk Greek yogurt, for garnish

seafood, meat, and poultry

Pan-Seared Halibut with Lemon Relish *51*

Grilled Lamb Chops with Lemon,
Sumac, and Za'atar *52*

Meyer Lemon Risotto with
Dungeness Crab, Tarragon,
and Crème Fraîche *54*

Cedar Plank–Grilled Salmon
with Lemons *56*

Grilled Flank Steak with Charred
Lemon Chimichurri *59*

Braised Beef with Preserved Lemons
and Harissa *61*

Toasted Bread and Chicken Salad
with Roasted Lemon-Shallot Vinaigrette *63*

Lemon Parmesan Chicken Soup
with Herbed Dumpling *66*

pan-seared halibut with *lemon relish*

The pulp and zest of a thin-skinned, medium-size lemon is the base of this piquant, chunky relish. Salty olives and capers balance the acidity, along with plenty of fresh parsley. Try it with other white-fleshed fish, grilled shrimp, or salmon, or with fresh sardines and anchovies. Note that the relish needs to marinate for four hours or up to overnight, so make it the day before you plan to cook the fish.

MAKES 4 SERVINGS

To make the relish, remove the pithy ends of the lemon quarters, and thinly slice the rest, discarding any seeds. Add the lemon slices to a bowl along with the shallots and salt. Cover and set aside for 45 minutes or until the lemons release some of their juice. Add the olives, capers, pepper flakes, and ¼ cup of the oil. In order for the flavors to develop fully, set the relish aside to marinate 4 hours or up to overnight.

Pat the halibut dry with a paper towel. In a small bowl, combine the fennel seed, salt, and pepper and sprinkle it all over the halibut. In a nonstick skillet or cast-iron pan over medium-high heat, heat the oil until it shimmers. Add the halibut and cook, undisturbed, until browned on the bottom, about 5 minutes. Flip, add the butter to the pan, and reduce the temperature to medium. Continue to cook, basting the halibut with the butter, for 2 minutes, or until the fish is opaque in the center.

Stir the parsley into the relish, spoon the relish over each piece of fish, and serve immediately.

FOR THE RELISH:

1 lemon, quartered (about ¾ cup)

2 small shallots, thinly sliced into rings (about ¼ cup)

1 teaspoon kosher salt

1 cup pitted, coarsely chopped green olives, such as Castelvetrano

2 tablespoons capers, rinsed and patted dry

½ teaspoon red pepper flakes

¼ cup extra-virgin olive oil

....

1½ pounds skinless halibut fillet, cut into 4 pieces

½ teaspoon fennel seed, freshly ground

½ teaspoon kosher salt

½ teaspoon freshly ground black pepper

2 tablespoons extra-virgin olive oil

2 tablespoons unsalted butter

¾ cup coarsely chopped flat-leaf parsley

grilled lamb chops *with* lemon, sumac, *and* za'atar

After marinating in plain yogurt gussied up with lemon, garlic, and mint, these lamb chops are coated with *za'atar* and sumac, Middle Eastern spices. Specifically, sumac is a pleasantly astringent, slightly fruity berry that is dried and ground. Together, they create an appealing, crispy crust on the chops when they meet the heat of the grill, perfectly complementing the lemony marinade. You can purchase both *za'atar* and sumac online and at well-stocked groceries or Middle Eastern markets. Note that the chops need to marinate overnight, so plan ahead.

MAKES 4 SERVINGS

1 (3 to 3½ pound) rack of lamb, rib bones frenched, or 3 pounds lamb loin chops, 1 to 1½ inches thick

Kosher salt and freshly ground black pepper

FOR THE MARINADE:

¾ cup plain whole milk yogurt

3 tablespoons extra-virgin olive oil

3 tablespoons freshly squeezed lemon juice

1 tablespoon finely chopped lemon zest

2 cloves garlic, finely minced

Pat the rack or chops dry with a paper towel, season them with salt and pepper, and lay them in a shallow nonreactive pan such as a rectangular glass baking dish.

In a small bowl, whisk together the yogurt, oil, lemon juice and zest, garlic, and mint. Pour the marinade over the chops, turning them once to coat both sides. Cover the pan with plastic wrap and refrigerate overnight.

Remove the lamb from the refrigerator 30 to 45 minutes prior to grilling to allow the meat to come to room temperature. Preheat a gas or charcoal grill for medium-high heat, about 350 degrees F. Remove the lamb from the marinade, wipe the marinade off completely with a paper towel, and discard it. Combine the oil, garlic, *za'atar*, and sumac, and use your fingers to rub the mixture all over the lamb.

Scrape the grate clean and lightly oil it. For a rack of lamb, turn one of the burners off, or bank the coals to one side of the grill. Lay the rack on the grate over direct heat and cook the lamb until browned all over, about 10 minutes. Move the lamb to a cooler part of the grill, cover and cook, turning occasionally, until an instant-read thermometer inserted in the center registers 130 degrees F, about 15 minutes. Let the lamb rest at least 10 minutes before cutting into individual chops.

For loin chops, lay the chops on the grate and grill for 3 minutes, then turn each chop 90 degrees, and cook for another 3 minutes, or until the chops are nicely charred. Flip the chops and cook them on the other side for about 6 more minutes, turning halfway through. They should still be pink inside. Transfer the chops to a warm plate to rest for 5 minutes before serving.

While the lamb rests, cut the lemons in half, lightly brush them with oil and grill, cut side down, until nicely charred, about 3 minutes. Arrange the lamb chops on a platter with the grilled lemons and mint leaves.

2 tablespoons coarsely
  chopped fresh mint

. . . .

3 tablespoons extra-virgin
  olive oil

2 cloves garlic, finely
  minced

3 tablespoons za'atar

4 teaspoons sumac

3 lemons, for garnish

Mint leaves, for garnish

meyer lemon risotto *with* dungeness crab, tarragon, *and* crème fraîche

This seafood risotto is my favorite way to celebrate our overlapping Dungeness crab and Meyer lemon seasons on the West Coast. On the East Coast, blue crabs or stone crabs would work nicely, as does king crab meat or whatever fresh, local option you can find. I incorporate a whole lemon, which accents the creamy rice and sweet crabmeat. If Meyer lemons are unavailable, use the finely chopped zest of a regular lemon and a squeeze of juice instead.

MAKES 6 SERVINGS

5 to 6 cups lightly flavored vegetable broth

1 Meyer lemon, peel removed with a vegetable peeler (reserve both the fruit and the peel)

2 tablespoons unsalted butter

2 tablespoons extra-virgin olive oil

1 small onion, cut into ½-inch dice (about 1 cup)

1 stalk green garlic, bulb and tender green parts finely chopped, or 1 large clove garlic, finely minced

1½ cups arborio rice

½ cup dry white wine or vermouth

8 ounces fresh crabmeat

In a large saucepan over medium heat, bring the broth to a simmer. Add the lemon peel and remove the pan from the heat. Cover and set aside.

In a heavy-bottomed pan over medium-low heat, melt the butter. When the butter is foamy, add the oil and onion and cook, stirring occasionally, until the onion is soft and translucent, about 5 minutes. Increase the heat to medium-high, add the garlic and rice, and stir until the rice smells slightly toasty, about 4 minutes. Add the wine and simmer, stirring occasionally, until it is reduced to a glaze, about 5 minutes. Add 1 cup of the warm broth, stir to cover the grains, and simmer, stirring frequently, until the broth is almost entirely absorbed before adding more. Repeat while continuing to stir until only about ½ cup of the broth remains, or the rice is creamy and cooked through, about 45 minutes. Reserve the broth.

Remove the peel from the broth and finely mince it. Section the lemon and finely chop the pulp, removing any seeds. Stir the peel and pulp into the rice and cook until they are warmed through, about 3 minutes. Stir in the crabmeat, cheese, and tarragon, adding a little bit of broth if necessary to loosen the risotto. When the cheese is melted and the crab is well distributed and warm, after about 3 minutes, stir in the crème fraîche. Serve immediately, garnished with the chives and tarragon leaves.

1 ounce Parmigiano-Reggiano cheese, finely grated (about ½ cup)

1 tablespoon coarsely chopped fresh tarragon, plus additional for garnish

¼ cup crème fraîche

¼ cup finely minced fresh chives

cedar plank–grilled salmon with lemons

I learned this technique for planked salmon from chef and restaurateur Vitaly Paley, when I worked on *The Paley's Place Cookbook*. Recipes for cooking on wood planks often call for soaking the board first, to prevent it from igniting. With this method, you *want* the plank to catch fire immediately. A tangle of thinly sliced spring vegetables, lemons, and dill flavors the salmon beneath it and protects the fish from burning. The result is a wonderfully smoky, moist piece of fish under a blanket of slightly crunchy, lightly charred vegetables. Note that a mandolin works best for slicing the vegetables and lemon, but if you don't have one, just slice them as thinly as possible.

MAKES 4 TO 6 SERVINGS

¼ cup light brown sugar

3 tablespoons kosher salt

½ chopped fresh dill, divided

1 tablespoon finely grated lemon zest

1 (2-pound) salmon fillet, or 6 (5½-ounce) center-cut fillets, skin on

1 (6-by-15-inch) cedar plank, or whatever size accommodates the length and width of your fish

5 tablespoons extra-virgin olive oil, divided, plus additional for brushing the plank

2 lemons, thinly sliced

In a small bowl, combine the sugar, salt, ¼ cup of the dill, and the zest. Pat the salmon dry with a paper towel and arrange it in a shallow glass baking dish and coat all over with the rub. Cover and refrigerate for 2 hours.

Preheat a gas grill for high heat, about 450 degrees F, or prepare a charcoal grill for direct-heat cooking over red-hot coals. Brush the plank generously with oil on both sides. Lay about two-thirds of the sliced lemons on the plank in a single layer.

Halve the remaining sliced lemons and add them to a medium bowl with the onion and fennel. Add 2 tablespoons of the oil and use your hands to toss the ingredients and coat them. Add the remaining ¼ cup dill, the fennel fronds, and a small pinch of salt.

Arrange the salmon on the plank over the lemons. Mound the vegetable mixture on the top and around the sides of the fish, covering the flesh. Drizzle the remaining 3 table-spoons oil on top. Place the plank on the grill; it should be hot enough to cause the plank to ignite. Let the plank burn around the fish (the lemons and vegetables will prevent the salmon from burning) and close the lid. Continue to cook until the thickest part of the fillet registers 130 to 135 degrees F on an instant-read thermometer, about 15 minutes depending on the thickness.

1 small spring or sweet onion, thinly sliced

1 small fennel bulb, thinly sliced

¼ cup lightly packed fennel fronds, coarsely chopped

grilled flank steak with charred lemon chimichurri

Chimichurri is Argentina's national steak sauce. A staple in the country's *parrillas* (steak houses), the silky green sauce can be as simple as olive oil flavored with dried oregano, red pepper flakes, and salt, or a more elaborate combination of herbs, spices, and garlic. My version includes finely chopped slices of grilled lemon for a pleasant hit of acidity and texture. The tangy sauce is a good accompaniment to thicker steaks, chicken, and fish, as long as they are grilled. Without the smoky char, whatever sits underneath the boldly flavored condiment is overshadowed. Note that the *chimichurri* needs to sit for at least two hours and up to overnight for the flavors to develop.

MAKES 4 SERVINGS

To make the *chimichurri*, trim the blossom and stem ends of the lemon, removing enough rind that the pulp shows. Cut the lemon into ¼-inch-thick slices and put them in a small bowl with the jalapeño. Toss with a little bit of oil and ¼ teaspoon of the salt, and grill or broil until lightly charred. Put the lemon slices and jalapeño back in the bowl and cover with a plate or plastic wrap. The steam will cause them to collapse slightly, making the skin of the jalapeño easy to remove.

Peel and seed the jalapeño (leave some seeds and the membrane if you want a spicy kick). Remove any seeds from the lemon slices. Put both ingredients in the bowl of a food processor and pulse several times to coarsely chop.

FOR THE *CHIMICHURRI*:

1 small lemon

1 small jalapeño

½ cup extra-virgin olive oil, plus additional for tossing ingredients and oiling the grill

1½ teaspoons kosher salt, divided

1 cup lightly packed flat-leaf parsley leaves

1 cup lightly packed fresh cilantro leaves

3 tablespoons fresh oregano leaves

2 cloves garlic, coarsely chopped

continued

1 tablespoon coarsely
    chopped shallot

1 tablespoon white wine
    vinegar

....

1 flank skirt or flatiron
    steak (about 1½ pounds)

Kosher salt and freshly
    ground black pepper

Add the remaining 1¼ teaspoons salt, the parsley, cilantro, oregano, garlic, shallot, and vinegar. Pulse the ingredients in short bursts, to chop and combine them without creating too fine a puree. With the motor running, drizzle in the oil. Remove the sauce to a medium bowl and let it sit for at least 2 hours or up to overnight. Taste for salt before serving, adding more if necessary.

Pat the steak dry with a paper towel and season it generously with salt and pepper. Preheat a gas grill for high heat, about 450 degrees F, or prepare a charcoal grill for direct-heat cooking over red-hot coals. Scrape the grate clean and lightly oil it. When the grill is hot, lay the steak on the grate. For rare to medium rare, cook for 3 minutes on one side, flip the steak, and cook for an additional 3 minutes on the other side (this may vary, depending on the size and thickness of the steak). Remove the steak from the grill and let it rest for at least 5 minutes before thinly slicing it against the grain.

To serve, lay the slices on a platter, drizzle them with any juices left over from slicing, and spoon some *chimichurri* over the top. Serve immediately and pass the remaining *chimichurri*.

braised beef *with* preserved lemons *and* harissa

Preserved lemons are an indispensable ingredient in the Moroccan kitchen. They find their way into fragrant tagines made with lamb, chicken, and beef, as well as fish and even salads. When I have time, I like to make this braise like a pot roast, using a cut of beef on the bone for extra flavor. A boneless cut or stew meat works beautifully too and cooks a bit more quickly. If you plan ahead, this tastes better every day it sits, the harissa, a North African chile paste, mellowing as it blends with the other flavors. Serve it with Toasted Cauliflower "Couscous" with Lemon, Parsley, and Almonds (page 25). You can find harissa at most well-stocked groceries or natural markets.

MAKES 4 TO 6 SERVINGS

Preheat the oven to 325 degrees F.

Pat the meat dry with a paper towel and season well with salt and pepper. In a Dutch oven or heavy, oven-proof pan with a lid, warm the oil over medium-high heat. Add the meat and sear it for 3 to 4 minutes on each side for a chuck roast, or brown the meat on all sides for stew meat. Be careful not to crowd the pan, browning in 2 batches if necessary.

Remove the browned beef from the pan to a large bowl. Add the onion to the pan and cook, stirring frequently to scrape up the brown bits on the bottom. After 3 or 4 minutes, or when the onion has softened slightly, add the lemon, garlic, *ras al hanout*, cumin, coriander, and harissa. Continue to cook for a few minutes, until the ingredients are aromatic.

- 1 (3-pound) bone-in chuck roast, or 2 pounds stew meat
- Kosher salt and freshly ground black pepper
- 3 tablespoons extra-virgin olive oil
- I medium onion, cut into large dice
- 1 Preserved Lemon (page 107) or store-bought, rinsed and finely chopped (peel only)
- 3 cloves garlic, finely chopped
- 1½ teaspoons *ras al hanout* (see note, page 62)
- 1 teaspoon cumin seeds, coarsely ground
- 1 teaspoon coriander seeds, coarsely ground

continued

1 to 3 tablespoons harissa, depending on your preferred heat level

3 cups beef stock or vegetable broth

2 sprigs fresh thyme

1 bay leaf

1 cup lightly packed, coarsely chopped flat-leaf parsley leaves

½ cup lightly packed, coarsely chopped cilantro leaves

Put the meat back in the pan, along with any juices in the bowl. Add the stock, thyme, and bay leaf, and bring the mixture to a boil. Carefully remove the pan from the heat, cover it with the lid, and put it in the oven.

Cook the beef for 2 hours (for stew meat) or 3 to 3½ hours for a larger, bone-in cut. Check the level of the stock occasionally, adding a little bit of water if the level is low or the pan or meat seems dry. The meat is ready when it is meltingly tender and has fallen off the bone. To serve, season to taste with additional salt and pepper, and add the parsley and cilantro.

NOTE: *Ras al hanout* is a North African spice blend. Find it online and at well-stocked groceries or Middle Eastern markets. To make your own, lightly toast and grind 1½ teaspoons coriander seeds, ¾ teaspoon cumin seeds, and ½ teaspoon red pepper flakes. Add 1¼ teaspoons ground cinnamon, 1 teaspoon sweet paprika, and ½ teaspoon each of ground cardamom, ground ginger, and turmeric.

toasted bread *and* chicken salad *with* roasted lemon-shallot vinaigrette

If this recipe seems familiar, perhaps you too are a fan of the legendary brick-oven roasted chicken with bread salad served at San Francisco's Zuni Café. That simple yet indescribably satisfying dish inspired this salad, right down to the currants, which round out the salad's flavors with their sweetness. During the summer, try tiny sweet cherry tomatoes, or roasted grapes in the fall.

I like to make a double batch of this vinaigrette so there's plenty left over to enjoy on salad greens, potatoes, grilled fish, and sliced tomatoes.

MAKES 4 TO 6 SERVINGS

Preheat the oven to 400 degrees F.

To make the vinaigrette, in a medium bowl, combine the lemon halves with the shallots and garlic. Toss them well with ¼ cup of the oil, 2 sprigs of the thyme, and 1 teaspoon of the salt and transfer them to a baking dish. Turn the lemons cut side down and distribute the ingredients in a single layer. Cover the pan with aluminum foil and roast, stirring occasionally, until the shallots are soft and caramelized, 45 to 55 minutes. Remove the pan from the oven and set aside to cool.

Increase the oven temperature to 425 degrees F. Toss the bread with the oil and season to taste with salt and pepper. Arrange the bread on a baking sheet in a single layer and toast for 10 to 12 minutes, or until lightly golden brown and still slightly chewy. Leave the oven on after toasting the bread.

FOR THE VINAIGRETTE:

1 lemon, halved

8 ounces shallots, peeled, halved if large

3 large cloves garlic, unpeeled

¾ cup extra-virgin olive oil, divided

4 sprigs fresh thyme, divided

2½ teaspoons kosher salt, divided

Juice of 1 lemon

. . . .

12 ounces peasant-style, rustic bread, roughly torn into 1-inch pieces (about 5 cups)

3 tablespoons extra-virgin olive oil

continued

Meanwhile, seed and coarsely chop the pulp from the roasted lemon halves, discarding the peel. Trim the root ends from the shallots, and peel the garlic. Add them all to a blender, along with the remaining 1½ teaspoons salt, the lemon juice, and any juices left in the baking dish. Blend until smooth and, with the blender running, slowly drizzle in the remaining ½ cup oil until the mixture is emulsified. Coarsely chop the thyme leaves from the remaining sprigs and add them to the blender. Pulse again to combine, and season to taste with pepper.

In a large bowl, toss the chicken with enough vinaigrette to moisten it. Add the toasted bread and more vinaigrette, until everything is lightly coated. Spread the contents of the bowl in a single layer on a baking sheet and place in the oven briefly to warm through, about 4 minutes.

Remove the pan from the oven, and turn the bread and chicken into a serving bowl or platter, along with the currants and greens. Toss well to combine, adding more vinaigrette to taste.

Freshly ground black pepper

4 cups leftover roast chicken, shredded or cut into bite-size pieces

3 tablespoons currants, plumped in warm water for 10 minutes and drained

4 cups lightly packed peppery greens, such as arugula, watercress, or small red mustard greens

lemon parmesan chicken soup
with herbed dumplings

Adding hard cheese rinds to stock is an Italian trick for making rich and unbeliev-ably delicious bases for soup and risotto. Coupled with lemon, chicken, and pillowy dumplings full of herbs, lemon zest, and more cheese, the soup is transformed into a satisfying meal. Make it in a wide pot or Dutch oven that can accommo-date a big batch of dumplings; almost everyone will ask for seconds.

MAKES 8 SERVINGS

1 (4 to 4½ pound) pastured chicken

5 carrots, divided

2 large leeks (about 1 pound), well rinsed

2 cloves garlic, smashed

2 stalks celery, cut into 2-inch pieces

1 small onion, peeled and halved

4 sprigs fresh thyme

2 bay leaves

2 teaspoons black peppercorns

Kosher salt and freshly ground black pepper

1 tablespoon unsalted butter

1 tablespoon extra-virgin olive oil

4 long strips lemon zest, removed with a vegetable peeler

Put the chicken in a large stockpot with 2 of the carrots, cut into large chunks; the green parts of the leeks, cut into 1-inch pieces; and the garlic, celery, onion, thyme, bay leaves, and peppercorns. Add enough cold water to cover the chicken. Bring to a boil over medium-high heat, reduce the heat to a simmer, and cook gently for 45 minutes to 1 hour, until the chicken is tender.

Transfer the chicken to a bowl to cool. When the chicken is cool enough to handle, gently pull it apart and remove the skin and bones from half of the bird, e.g. a thigh, a leg and wing, and half of the breast meat. Discard the skin, add the bones back to the stockpot, and reserve the chicken for the soup. Refrigerate the rest of the chicken in an airtight container for another use, such as Toasted Bread and Chicken Salad with Roasted Lemon-Shallot Vinaigrette (page 63). Continue to simmer the stock until it is reduced by one-third, about 1 hour. Strain it through a fine-mesh sieve into a large bowl, discarding the solids. You should have 8 to 10 cups of stock. Season it with salt and pepper to taste.

In a wide pot or Dutch oven over medium-high heat, warm the butter and oil. Add the whites of the leeks, halved and cut into ½-inch pieces, and the remaining carrots, cut into ¼-inch-thick coins. Sauté for several minutes before adding the zest, rinds, and stock. Reduce the heat and gently simmer the soup while you make the dumplings.

To make the dumplings, in a medium bowl, whisk together the flour, baking powder, salt, pepper, zest, herbs, and cheese. Make a well in the center, and add the milk and eggs, whisking them together and incorporating the flour as you go. Switch to a wooden spoon and slowly stir in the butter until the ingredients are well incorporated. At this point, the dough should be loose enough to stir easily, but not mushy. Scrape the sides of the bowl with a spatula while mixing, to incorporate all of the dry ingredients. Resist the urge to overmix, even though the dough looks like a wet shaggy mass.

Using 2 teaspoons, form the dough into dumplings, lowering them directly into the simmering soup all at once. Cover the pot and simmer the dumplings for 5 minutes before checking to see if they've floated to the top. If so, turn them over, add the reserved chicken, and continue to simmer until the dumplings are cooked through and the chicken is warmed through, about 10 minutes. Serve immediately and continue to enjoy leftovers for the next 2 to 3 days.

1 medium Parmigiano-Reggiano cheese rind (about 6 ounces)

FOR THE DUMPLINGS:

2 cups unbleached all-purpose flour

2 teaspoons baking powder

2 teaspoons kosher salt

1 teaspoon freshly ground black pepper

2 teaspoons finely chopped lemon zest

¼ cup coarsely chopped soft fresh herbs, such as tarragon, chives, and parsley

½ ounce Parmigiano-Reggiano cheese, finely grated (about ¼ cup)

1 cup whole milk

2 eggs, lightly beaten

¼ cup (½ stick) unsalted butter, melted and cooled slightly

sweets

Mini Lemon Meringue Whoopie Pies
with Lemon Curd Filling *71*

Best Lemon Bars *73*

Lemon and Poppy Seed Parfait
with Strawberries *75*

Chocolate-Filled Lemon
Almond Macarons *78*

Lemon Crinkle Cookies *80*

Lemon Buttermilk Panna Cotta with Lemon
Verbena and Blackberries *83*

Affogato with Limoncello Ice Cream *85*

Lemon Crème Brulée with
Lavender and Honey *87*

Toasted Coconut–Lemon Tart *90*

Meyer Lemon and Tangerine
Olive Oil Cake *92*

mini lemon meringue whoopie pies with lemon curd filling

Inspired by lemon meringue pie, I added brown sugar to these meringues to approximate the pie's toasty flavor. A half recipe of Lemon Curd will leave you with three egg whites, just the right amount for a batch of these meringues.

After assembling them, I recommend letting the cookies sit for several hours at room temperature or—better yet—overnight after assembling them; the texture approximates something between the pie that inspires them and the spongy, cakelike texture of a traditional whoopie pie. And it only gets better, if you can make them last.

MAKES ABOUT 2 DOZEN WHOOPIE PIES

Preheat the oven to 200 degrees F. Line 2 baking sheets with parchment paper.

Put the granulated and brown sugars in the bowl of a food processor. Pulse in short bursts until they are well incorporated and finely ground. Set aside.

Put the egg whites in the clean, dry bowl of a stand mixer fitted with the whisk attachment, or a clean, dry bowl that can be used with an electric handheld mixer. (If there's even a speck of egg yolk, oil, or water in the bowl or the whites, they won't stiffen.) Begin mixing on medium-low speed. When the whites are frothy, add the cream of tartar and salt and continue beating for about 2 minutes, or until the whites are thick and foamy. Increase the speed

½ cup granulated sugar

¼ cup light brown sugar

3 egg whites, at room temperature

¼ teaspoon cream of tartar

Pinch kosher salt

½ teaspoon vanilla extract

⅔ cup (½ recipe) Lemon Curd (page 109)

continued

to medium-high and add the sugar mixture slowly, about 1 tablespoon at a time. When all the sugar is incorporated, increase the speed to high, whipping until stiff, shiny peaks form, about 10 minutes. Add the vanilla and beat until just blended, about 5 seconds.

Spoon the meringue into a pastry bag fitted with a plain ½-inch tip or a ziplock bag with one corner snipped off. Hold the bag perpendicular to the baking sheets and pipe small flat disks, about 1¼ inches in diameter and ¼ inch high. Bake until the meringues are dry and crisp, about 1½ hours. Turn off the oven and leave them there to cool completely.

To assemble the cookies, arrange half of the meringues flat side up on a baking sheet. Put the chilled curd in a clean pastry bag fitted with a plain ½-inch tip or another ziplock bag with one corner snipped off. Pipe about 2 teaspoons onto each meringue. Gently press the remaining meringues flat side down onto the curd. As they sit, the meringues will become softer and chewier.

best lemon bars

Lemon lovers love lemon bars, and there are lots of recipes to prove it. For me, the best lemon bar has a topping-to-crust ratio of 2:1, with a fat layer of curdlike topping that hovers between tart and sweet. If that's your definition of a perfect lemon bar too, look no further. Reduce the time between cooling and consumption by putting the pan in the freezer for thirty minutes after baking. These bars cut beautifully in a semifrozen state.

MAKES 2 DOZEN (1½-BY-3-INCH) BARS

Preheat the oven to 350 degrees F. Line a 9-by-13-inch baking pan with foil and lightly coat the foil with cooking spray or melted butter.

To make the crust, in a small bowl, stir together the flour and salt. Using a stand mixer fitted with the paddle attachment or a handheld electric mixer, beat the butter and sugar on medium speed until it is light in color and fluffy, about 3 minutes. Add the zest and vanilla and mix to incorporate. Reduce to low speed and add the flour mixture, using a spatula to scrape the bottom and sides of the bowl several times. Stop mixing when the ingredients are fully incorporated but still crumbly. Do not overmix or the crust will be difficult to distribute in the pan.

continued

FOR THE CRUST:

2½ cups unbleached all-purpose flour

¾ teaspoon kosher salt

1 cup (2 sticks) unsalted butter, at room temperature

¾ cup sugar

2 teaspoons finely chopped lemon zest

1 teaspoon vanilla extract

FOR THE TOPPING:

6 eggs, lightly beaten

2 cups sugar

¼ cup plus 1 tablespoon unbleached all-purpose flour

1 cup freshly squeezed
   lemon juice (from
   4 medium lemons)

1 tablespoon plus
   2 teaspoons finely
   chopped lemon zest
   (from 2 small lemons)

½ cup whole milk

½ teaspoon kosher salt

....

Confectioners' sugar,
   for serving

Pour the crumbly dough into the prepared pan and use your fingers to distribute it evenly over the bottom, lightly pressing it down and making sure to bring the dough up the sides of the pan slightly, to contain the topping. Bake until toasty brown, about 25 minutes.

Meanwhile, make the topping. In a large bowl, whisk the eggs with the sugar and flour. Stir in the lemon juice and zest, milk, and salt.

When the crust is done, reduce the oven temperature to 325 degrees F. Stir the topping ingredients together again before pouring the topping over the warm crust. Place the pan in the middle of the oven and bake until the topping feels firm when lightly touched, about 20 minutes. Cool the pan on a wire rack for at least 30 minutes or to room temperature before cutting the bars. Dust generously with confectioners' sugar before serving.

lemon and poppy seed parfait with strawberries

This parfait is a play on the classic British dessert, Eton mess. I fold poppy seed–speckled meringues into whipped cream streaked with ribbons of lemon curd, then freeze the whole "mess." The sticky, chewy magic that happens when meringue and cream are frozen is further improved with strawberries and fresh mint. Note that you need to make the curd before the meringues, so it has time to cool.

MAKES 6 TO 8 SERVINGS

Preheat the oven to 200 degrees F. Put the sugar in a pie tin or small pan with sides and warm in the oven for 10 minutes. Line a baking sheet with parchment paper and set aside.

To make the meringues, place the egg whites in the clean, dry bowl of a stand mixer fitted with the whisk attachment, or a clean, dry bowl that can be used with an electric handheld mixer. (If there's even a speck of egg yolk, oil, or water in the bowl or the whites, they won't stiffen.) Begin mixing on medium-low speed, adding a pinch of salt when the whites are frothy. Continue beating for about 2 minutes, or until the whites are thick and foamy. Increase the speed to medium-high and begin adding the warm sugar slowly, 1 tablespoon at a time. When all the sugar is incorporated, increase the speed to high, whipping until stiff, shiny peaks form, about 10 minutes. With a spatula, gently fold in the poppy seeds.

Dollop the meringue onto the prepared baking sheet, making 6 mounds and using the back of a spoon to flatten

FOR THE MERINGUES:

¾ cup superfine sugar

3 egg whites, at room temperature

Pinch kosher salt

1 tablespoon poppy seeds

....

2 cups heavy cream

⅔ cup (½ recipe) Lemon Curd (page 109)

2 pints fresh strawberries, hulled and halved or quartered

3 tablespoons sugar

2 tablespoons freshly squeezed lemon juice

3 to 4 fresh mint leaves

continued

the tops slightly. Bake the meringues until dry and crisp, about 1½ hours. Wash and dry the mixer bowl and whisk and place them in the refrigerator.

Line a 9-by-5-by-3-inch loaf pan with plastic wrap, leaving enough overhang on all sides to cover the top of the parfait and make lifting it out of the pan easier. Set aside.

To assemble the parfait, add the cream to the chilled mixer bowl, or use a whisk with a chilled, nonreactive bowl. Whip the cream on medium speed, or by hand, until soft peaks form. Using a spatula, fold in the lemon curd without combining it completely, just until the mixture is streaky. Break the meringues into chunks ranging in size from large crumbs to walnut halves. Fold them into the cream, stirring gently to distribute. Spoon the mixture into the prepared pan, cover the top with plastic wrap, and freeze for at least 4 hours before serving.

Meanwhile, in a medium bowl, toss the strawberries with the sugar and lemon juice and allow them to sit for 30 minutes, or until a syrup forms. Cut the mint leaves lengthwise into thin strips and toss with the berries; there should be only a suggestion of mint, so keep the amount minimal.

To serve, use the overhanging plastic wrap to lift the parfait out of the pan. Cut the parfait into 1 to 1½-inch slices and spoon the berries over the top.

VARIATION: Substitute 2 teaspoons rose water for the poppy seeds, and raspberries for the strawberries. Garnish each plate with a few rose petals.

chocolate-filled lemon almond macarons

If the world were divided into lemon people and chocolate people, I'd join the lemon team. If you're on the fence or don't want to choose, this is the cookie for you. Lemon and chocolate seem like an unlikely combination until you try them together. You can also sandwich Lemon Curd (page 109) between these macarons or white chocolate ganache flavored with a touch of orange flower water.

MAKES 2 DOZEN MACARONS

1½ cups confectioners' sugar

1⅓ cups almond flour

1 tablespoon finely grated lemon zest

4 egg whites, at room temperature

Pinch of cream of tartar

¼ cup granulated sugar

FOR THE FILLING:

½ cup plus 2 tablespoons heavy cream

2 teaspoons coarsely chopped lemon zest

Pinch kosher salt

6 ounces bittersweet chocolate, finely chopped (about 1 cup)

1 tablespoon unsalted butter

2 tablespoons freshly squeezed lemon juice

Line 2 baking sheets with parchment paper. In a medium bowl, combine the confectioners' sugar, flour, and zest, and set aside.

In the clean, dry bowl of a stand mixer fitted with the whisk attachment, or a clean, dry bowl that can be used with a handheld electric mixer, beat the egg whites on medium speed until frothy. Add the cream of tartar and continue to beat until the whites hold soft peaks. Increase the speed to medium high, slowly add the granulated sugar, and beat until the whites hold firm, glossy peaks. Stop before they are stiff and shiny.

Sift one-third of the flour mixture over the whites and use a spatula to gently fold it in. Repeat with half of the remaining flour mixture, mixing to incorporate before adding the remaining flour mixture. The batter should be loose, but hold its shape.

Spoon the batter into a pastry bag fitted with a plain ½-inch tip or a ziplock bag with one corner snipped off. Holding the bag perpendicular to the prepared baking sheets, pipe small mounds, about 1 inch in diameter and ¼ inch high, 1 inch apart. Let the dough rest for 20 minutes, or until the macarons are no longer sticky to the touch. Meanwhile, preheat the oven to 350 degrees F.

Bake the macarons for 12 to 16 minutes, rotating the pan once during baking. They will puff, become shiny, and fall very slightly. When fully baked, they will be dry and very lightly brown. Remove the pans to a rack and let the cookies cool completely on the pans while you make the filling.

To make the filling, in a small pan over medium heat, heat the cream with the zest and salt to just below the boiling point. Put the chocolate in a small bowl and pour the hot cream over it. Let it for sit several minutes to melt the chocolate before adding the butter and stirring until smooth. Stir in the lemon juice.

To assemble the cookies, turn half of them upside down. Use an offset spatula or small knife to spread each half with about 2 teaspoons of the filling, leaving the edges uncovered. Top with the remaining cookies, pressing together gently so the filling spreads to the edges of the sandwich.

lemon crinkle cookies

Once upon a time, these cookies were chocolate. We made them at Wildwood, the restaurant (now closed) that brought me to Portland. A fan of their chewy texture, I thought it would be fun to make them in other flavors. Since creating the chocolate version of a recipe is often as easy as substituting cocoa powder for some of the flour, I did the reverse, removing some of the cocoa and replacing it with the same weight in flour. And it worked! A quick roll in powdered sugar before baking gives these cookies their crinkly, crackly appearance.

MAKES 4 DOZEN COOKIES

1½ cups unbleached all-purpose flour

¼ cup cornstarch

1½ teaspoons baking powder

½ teaspoon kosher salt

1 cup granulated sugar

2 tablespoons finely grated lemon zest (from 2 medium lemons)

½ cup (1 stick) unsalted butter, at room temperature

2 eggs

¼ teaspoon lemon extract (optional)

½ cup confectioners' sugar

Line 2 baking sheets with parchment paper. In a small bowl, whisk together the flour, cornstarch, baking powder, and salt. Set aside.

In the bowl of a stand mixer fitted with the paddle attachment, or a bowl you'd use with a handheld electric mixer, combine the sugar and zest. Using your fingers, rub the zest with the sugar until it is very aromatic. Add the butter and beat on medium speed until well incorporated. Using a spatula, scrape the bottom and sides of the bowl, then increase the speed to medium high, mixing until the butter and sugar are light in color and fluffy. Add the eggs one at a time, mixing well between additions. Add the lemon extract, followed by the dry ingredients. Mix on low speed just until blended, without any floury streaks.

Preheat the oven to 325 degrees F. Put the confectioners' sugar in a shallow, wide bowl, or a pie plate. Use a tablespoon to scoop up a spoonful of dough about the size of small cherry tomato. Dust your hands with confectioners' sugar, form the dough into a ball, and roll the ball in the sugar until well covered. Place the balls on the prepared baking sheets, leaving 1 inch on all sides.

Bake the cookies for 5 minutes, rotate the pan, and bake for another 5 to 7 minutes. When they are ready, the cookies will be set around the edges and slightly puffed. The centers will be soft, but not shiny. Place the baking sheets on a rack to cool for 15 minutes, then move the cookies from the pans onto the rack to cool completely.

VARIATION: If you want to try the original, substitute ⅔ cup unsweetened Dutch-processed cocoa powder for ½ cup of the all-purpose flour and 2 tablespoons of the cornstarch.

lemon buttermilk panna cotta with lemon verbena and blackberries

Panna cotta is a simple yet elegant dessert. A creamy canvas for creative combinations of flavors and textures, this version is redolent of lemon and tangy buttermilk. My favorite seasonal fruits for pairing with silky panna cotta include spring strawberries and sweet Rainier cherries, summer cane berries and stone fruit, and fall plums and figs.

Note that the panna cotta needs to firm up for least six hours, or overnight, so make this dish the day before you'd like to serve it. If you don't plan to turn it out of the dish, you can eat the panna cotta sooner, after two to three hours.

MAKES 8 SERVINGS

Lightly coat 8 (6-ounce) ramekins or dishes with a neutral-flavored oil such as canola and set aside.

In a large saucepan over medium heat, combine the cream, ½ cup plus 2 tablespoons of the sugar, the zest, and lemon verbena, stirring until the sugar dissolves. Remove the pan from the heat, cover, and infuse the cream for 30 minutes, or until the lemon flavors are pronounced. In a small bowl, soften the gelatin in 1 tablespoon of cold water for about 5 minutes, then stir it into the warm cream. When the gelatin has dissolved, add the buttermilk and stir well. Strain the mixture through a fine-mesh sieve into a container with a spout, such as a large measuring cup, and pour it into the prepared ramekins. Cover them with plastic wrap and refrigerate until firm, at least 6 hours, or overnight.

2⅔ cups heavy cream

1 cup sugar, divided

2 tablespoons zest, removed with a zester (from 2 medium lemons)

¼ cup lightly packed lemon verbena leaves, plus 8 for garnish

1 tablespoon plus 1 teaspoon powdered gelatin

1½ cups buttermilk

4 cups fresh blackberries (about 2 pints)

1 tablespoon freshly squeezed lemon juice

continued

Before serving, put the remaining 6 tablespoons of sugar in a blender or food processor with 1 cup of the blackberries and puree. Strain the puree through a fine-mesh sieve and combine with the remaining berries and lemon juice, adding more juice to taste.

To serve, unmold the ramekins by running a thin paring knife around the sides or dipping the ramekin in warm water to loosen the panna cotta. Put a small plate or bowl over the ramekin, flip it over, and shake vigorously to loosen. Spoon the blackberries and sauce around the base of the panna cotta. Garnish the top with a lemon verbena leaf.

Lemon verbena can be found at some farmers' markets, but it's easy to grow in a pot at home. Harvest any remaining leaves in the fall to dry for tea. Lemon thyme and lavender make good substitutes, or you can skip the herbal element altogether.

affogato with limoncello ice cream

This decadent, sippable adult dessert is a riff on an Italian favorite: it's essentially an *affogato* (the Italian word for "drowned"), but instead of pouring a shot of espresso over the mascarpone-enriched limoncello ice cream, I call for shaking the two together in a cocktail shaker. Serve it with a spoon and a straw, for slurping up the dregs.

MAKES 6 SERVINGS

In a medium saucepan over medium-high heat, bring the cream and milk to a simmer with ½ cup of the sugar, the salt, and lemon peel. Remove the pan from the heat, cover, and set aside for 20 minutes to infuse.

Meanwhile, in a medium nonreactive bowl, whisk the yolks with the remaining ¼ cup of sugar until smooth, and set aside. Prepare an ice bath for the custard by filling a large bowl halfway with ice and cold water and setting it in the sink.

When the cream mixture is infused, return it to the stove over medium heat until it is hot, but not boiling. Slowly add a ladleful of cream to the yolk mixture, whisking constantly until smooth (this is called tempering the yolks, a technique used to prevent them from curdling when they are combined with the hot milk). Repeat one more time, then pour the yolk mixture back into the saucepan over medium-low heat. Stir the custard constantly with a wooden spoon or heatproof spatula, scraping the bottom as you stir, until it reaches 170 degrees F

continued

2 cups heavy cream

¾ cup whole milk

¾ cup sugar, divided

½ teaspoon kosher salt

Peel of 1 lemon

5 egg yolks

¼ cup mascarpone cheese

½ teaspoon vanilla extract

⅓ cup Homemade Limoncello (page 100) or store-bought

6 shots espresso, at room temperature

6 lemon twists, for garnish

on an instant-read thermometer and coats the spoon or spatula. Remove the pan from the heat and whisk in the mascarpone and vanilla. Pour the custard through a fine-mesh sieve into a clean medium bowl. Place the bowl in the prepared ice bath to cool, and chill in the refrigerator until completely cold, at least 3 hours, or up to overnight.

When the custard is cold, whisk in the limoncello and freeze the mixture in an ice cream maker according to the manufacturer's instructions.

To serve, place a scoop of ice cream in a cocktail shaker or a glass jar with a lid. Add a shot of espresso and shake vigorously. Pour into a cocktail glass and garnish with a lemon twist. Repeat for each serving.

lemon crème brulée with lavender and honey

I know I'm not alone in finding childlike pleasure in the act of breaking through the crisp sugar crust of a crème brulée. Here, lemon and lavender perfume the honey-sweetened custard under the bruléed top, creating a tried and true trio of flavors. Lavender can be potent, and different varieties have different strengths; be sure to taste the cream as it infuses, so that the flavors are balanced.

MAKES 6 SERVINGS

Preheat the oven to 300 degrees F.

In a heavy saucepan, combine the cream, honey, lemon zest, lavender, and salt. Bring the mixture to a gentle simmer over medium heat, cover, and remove from the heat. Steep 10 minutes and taste the cream to determine if the lemon and lavender flavors are balanced and to your liking. When they are, strain the mixture, discard the zest and lavender, and return the cream to the pot. If it has cooled completely, warm the cream over medium heat until it is hot, but not boiling.

Meanwhile, in a medium bowl, whisk the yolks and egg together with the sugar until smooth. Slowly add some of the warm cream to the yolks, about ½ cup at a time, whisking constantly to keep the eggs from curdling. After adding 1 cup of cream, pour the tempered yolk mixture back into the pan with the remaining cream. Add the vanilla and strain the mixture into

continued

2 cups heavy cream

2 tablespoons honey

3 tablespoons coarsely chopped lemon zest (from 3 medium lemons)

2 tablespoons fresh lavender flowers (or 4 teaspoons dried)

⅛ teaspoon salt

3 yolks

1 egg

¼ cup granulated sugar, plus additional for caramelizing

1 teaspoon vanilla extract

another container to cool in an ice bath for baking later, or divide it between 6 (4-ounce) ramekins or glass custard cups.

Arrange the dishes in a deep baking pan and fill the pan with enough hot water to come halfway up the sides of the dishes. Put the baking pan in the oven and bake until the custard is set around edges and slightly jiggly in center, about 40 minutes. Remove the pan from the oven and allow the custards to cool before covering with plastic wrap. Store in the refrigerator to cool completely, 3 hours to overnight.

Just before serving, sprinkle the top of each custard with a thin, even coating of sugar. Place the dishes under a preheated broiler for 2 to 3 minutes, or until the sugar melts, or use a hand-held blowtorch to caramelize the sugar.

toasted coconut–lemon tart

We used to have this tart after Easter dinner. After not tasting it for many years, I asked my mom for the recipe, which came from her sister, my Aunt Betty. It wasn't as good as my memory of it—overly sweet and not nearly lemony enough. Still, I knew I wanted to revive it. The recipe below bears little resemblance to the original; it's much better. We all agree that it's time to reintroduce the tart at the family Easter table, or any spring celebration.

Note that the dough needs to chill for two hours, so plan accordingly. It can also be made ahead and refrigerated up to three days.

MAKES ONE 10-INCH TART

FOR THE CRUST:

1¼ cups unbleached all-purpose flour

½ cup confectioners' sugar

2 tablespoons cornstarch

¼ teaspoon kosher salt

10 tablespoons (1¼ sticks) unsalted butter, cold, cut into small pieces

¼ teaspoon vanilla extract

FOR THE FILLING:

1 cup sugar

2 tablespoons finely chopped lemon zest (from 2 medium lemons)

2 tablespoons cornstarch

To make the crust, in the bowl of a stand mixer fitted with the paddle attachment, combine the flour, confectioners' sugar, cornstarch, and salt. Add the butter all at once and mix on low speed until the ingredients begin to come together to make a cohesive dough; this will take a bit of time, as long as 7 to 10 minutes. Just before the dough looks like it's ready to form a ball, add the vanilla and mix to combine. Shape the ball of dough into a disk, wrap it in plastic wrap, and refrigerate until firm, about 2 hours.

On a lightly floured surface, roll out the pastry to make a 12- to 13-inch circle. Fit the dough into a 10-inch fluted tart pan, prick the dough all over with a fork, and freeze it for 30 minutes. While the dough freezes, preheat the oven to 350 degrees F and place a rack in the bottom third of the oven.

Place the frozen crust on a baking sheet and bake, uncovered, for about 15 minutes. (There's no need to cover the crust or use pie weights.) Rotate the pan and bake for another 10 minutes, or until the crust is lightly golden. Place the baking sheet on a rack to cool the crust and reduce the oven temperature to 325 degrees F.

While the crust cools, make the filling. In a medium bowl, combine the sugar and zest and use your fingers to rub the two together until the sugar is fragrant. Stir in the cornstarch and salt. In a separate smaller bowl, whisk the eggs with the yolks, then whisk in the butter and lemon juice. Whisk the egg and butter mixture into the sugar mixture, beating vigorously to combine. Stir in the coconut.

Pour the mixture into the cooled crust. Bake for 20 minutes on the bottom rack, rotating the pan and keeping an eye on the coconut; if it's getting too dark, cover the top loosely with a piece of aluminum foil. Bake for 20 more minutes, or until the filling sets up around the edges and is slightly jiggly in the center. Cool to room temperature before serving.

½ teaspoon kosher salt

2 eggs

2 egg yolks

¼ cup (½ stick) unsalted butter, melted and cooled

3 tablespoons freshly squeezed lemon juice

1½ cups lightly packed unsweetened, dried coconut flakes (also called coconut chips)

meyer lemon and *tangerine olive oil cake*

I've made an olive oil cake with whole oranges for my husband's birthday longer than either of us can remember. He was born in January, when citrus fruit is plentiful, and I've often thought about substituting Meyer lemons or blood oranges for the navel oranges in my recipe. Not wanting to meddle with tradition, I only recently got around to creating this version. A mash-up of a couple of favorite simple cake recipes, this one has cornmeal, which also makes it a good candidate for breakfast in my book.

MAKES ONE 10-INCH CAKE

3½ cups sugar, divided

2 Meyer lemons, preferably organic

2 small tangerines

1⅔ cups unbleached all-purpose flour

1 cup polenta or medium-grind cornmeal

1 tablespoon baking powder

½ teaspoon kosher salt

4 eggs

⅔ cup extra-virgin olive oil

Lightly sweetened whipped cream, for serving

In a medium saucepan, combine 2 cups of the sugar with 2 cups of water. Bring the mixture to a boil over medium-high heat. Add the lemons and tangerines once the sugar has dissolved. (The fruits should be submerged by two-thirds in the simple syrup. If they aren't, add more water.) Reduce the heat to a simmer, cover the pan, and gently poach the fruits until they are very tender, 20 to 30 minutes. Transfer them to a plate to cool.

Preheat the oven to 350 degrees F and lightly oil a 10-inch cake pan. Line the bottom with parchment paper and set aside.

When the fruits have cooled, slice off their ends, and quarter them. Remove any seeds or large pieces of membrane, add the pulp to the bowl of a food processor, and process until fairly smooth. You should have about 1¼ cups puree. Set aside.

In a small bowl, stir together the flour, polenta, baking powder, and salt, and set aside.

Put the eggs in the bowl of a stand mixer fitted with the whisk attachment, or use a handheld electric mixer on high speed to whip the eggs until they are foamy and lighter in color, about 2 minutes. With the mixer running, slowly add the remaining 1½ cups sugar and continue to whip on high speed until the mixture is thick and creamy white, about 4 minutes. Reduce the speed to medium and drizzle in the oil. Add the pureed fruit and mix to combine. Remove the mixing bowl and fold in one-third of the flour mixture. When the batter is smooth, add the rest of the flour. Pour the batter into the prepared pan and smooth the top with a spatula.

Bake until the cake is dark golden brown and springs back after being lightly pressed in the middle, 50 to 60 minutes. Let it cool on a rack for 15 minutes before removing it from the pan. Let it cool completely before slicing and serving with a dollop of lightly sweetened whipped cream.

drinks

Rose Geranium Lemonade *97*

Strawberry Lemon Agua Fresca
with Basil *98*

Lemon Mint Limonina *99*

Homemade Limoncello *100*

Lemon Stick for Adults *101*

Green-and-Lemon Shots *102*

Lemon Rosemary Barley Water *103*

rose geranium lemonade

Lemonade from scratch is a labor of love, but I assure you it's worth the effort. The trick is to use the lemon peels to make a syrup to add to the juice. Mix the resulting elixir with still or sparkling water and pour it all over ice. Consider adding a splash of vodka or gin. Note that the sugar needs to infuse overnight for the best flavor.

MAKES A SCANT QUART OF SYRUP TO YIELD 2 TO 2½ QUARTS LEMONADE

Using a vegetable peeler, remove the peels of the lemons in wide strips, reserving the lemons. Place the strips in a 2-quart jar or a nonreactive, lidded pitcher with the rose geranium leaves. Add the sugar and, using a muddler or the back of a wooden spoon, mash the peels and leaves with the sugar to release their essential oils. When the peels are coated with sugar, cover the jar and let sit overnight at room temperature. The next day, the sugar will be wet, and the contents will be sitting slightly lower in the jar.

Juice the reserved lemons; you should get about 2 cups of juice. If you're slightly short, add enough water to make 2 cups. Add the juice to the sugar and peels, cover, and shake the jar vigorously to dissolve the sugar and combine it with the lemon juice. Taste the syrup. The flavor of the rose geranium should be subtle. If it is to your liking, strain the syrup through a fine-mesh sieve into a clean jar and store it in the refrigerator. (For additional flavor, add a few more leaves and let the jar sit overnight in the refrigerator before straining the syrup.)

To make lemonade, pour equal parts syrup and water in a tall glass. Take a sip and add more water or syrup to taste. Serve over ice, garnished with a few flowers.

8 medium lemons

½ cup lightly packed rose geranium leaves, (7 to 10 small leaves)

2 cups superfine sugar

Rose geranium flowers, for garnish

Rose geranium is an old-fashioned flavor, perfect for lemonade. It can be difficult to find unless you grow it yourself, or have a reliable source. Most nurseries carry scented geraniums, or you can go with a different herbal addition—lavender, basil, lemon verbena, and rosemary are other favorites.

strawberry lemon agua fresca with basil

Agua fresca is one of the most invigorating ways to enjoy fresh fruit (and some-times vegetables) in season. Pureed ripe fruit, water, and a small amount of sweetener are combined with herbs and lemon or lime juice, and served over ice. I like to use a combination of still and sparkling water. Occasionally I'll swap out the strawberries here for the same amount of cucumber.

MAKES ABOUT 2½ QUARTS AGUA FRESCA

1 lemon

½ cup sugar

4 cups ripe strawberries, stemmed and halved (about 1 pound)

1 cup lightly packed fresh basil leaves

Using a vegetable peeler, remove the lemon peel and place the peels in a large nonreactive pitcher or 4-quart jar with the sugar. Using a muddler or the back of a wooden spoon, mash the peels with the sugar to release their essential oils. Set aside.

Trim the blossom and stem ends of the lemon, removing enough rind that the pulp shows. Using a sharp paring knife, cut away the white pith and chop the pulp into small pieces, removing the seeds as you go.

Puree the lemon pulp, strawberries, and basil leaves in a blender with enough water to loosen the mixture, about ½ cup. Strain through a fine-mesh sieve into the pitcher with the peels and sugar, adding at least as much cold water as you have puree, starting with 5 cups. Stir the liquid with the sugar until it has dissolved, taste, and add more sugar and water to taste. The agua fresca should be light, refreshing, and barely sweet. Serve over crushed ice.

lemon mint limonina

Variations on this refreshing slushie are enjoyed around the globe, but the Israeli version—the limonana—seems to be the best known. I learned about the drink from my friend Nina, who became obsessed with a similar drink made with limes when she lived in Thailand. Occasionally she'd have the street vendors who made them throw in some ginger.

This drink is named for Nina, who lives in Mumbai now. It's made with whole, peeled lemons and mint, an essential herb in Indian cooking. The two are whirred together in a blender with crushed ice and ginger simple syrup, which is what makes it the limonina-with-an-*i*.

MAKES 1 SERVING

In a small saucepan, combine the sugar with 1 cup of water. Bring the mixture to a boil over medium-high heat, stirring occasionally. When the sugar has dissolved, add the ginger and remove the pan from the heat. Leave the ginger in the simple syrup and let it cool completely. If you're only making 1 or 2 limonina, you'll have syrup left over. Use it to sweeten hot or cold tea, or add a splash to sparkling water or lemonade. It will keep several weeks.

Meanwhile, trim the blossom and stem ends of the lemons, removing enough rind that the pulp shows. Using a sharp paring knife, cut away the peel and white pith. Set the peel aside for another use. Cut the pulp into small pieces, removing the seeds as you go.

Put the lemon pulp in a blender with the mint, ½ cup of the ginger syrup, and some of the grated ginger, and the ice. Blend until slushy, adding water if necessary to sip this drink through a straw.

1 cup sugar

1-inch knob ginger, peeled and coarsely grated

2 small lemons

⅓ cup packed fresh mint leaves

1½ cups crushed ice or about 7 ice cubes

homemade limoncello

Limoncello is a liqueur produced primarily in southern Italy, where Sorrento lemons grow. After steeping the peels in neutral spirits or vodka, Italians add a simple syrup made with varying amounts of sugar and water (or milk) and continue to age the mixture in the freezer. Limoncello is typically served well chilled, usually after a meal as a digestif. Note that the limoncello will need to age for at least two weeks.

MAKES ABOUT 8 CUPS LIMONCELLO

10 lemons, preferably organic

1 (750 ml) bottle 100 proof vodka

3 cups sugar

Using a vegetable peeler, remove the peel from the lemons in wide strips, cutting away any pith remaining on the peel. Set the fruit aside for another use. Put the peels in a large nonreactive container and pour the bottle of vodka over them. Cover the container with plastic wrap and store it in a cool, dark spot for as long as you can wait, at least 2 weeks and preferably 4 weeks.

In a medium saucepan, bring 4 cups of water to a boil with the sugar, stirring constantly until the sugar dissolves. Remove the pan from the heat and cool completely. Add the sugar syrup to the vodka, cover, and let the limoncello sit for 24 hours. Strain the mixture into a clean 2-quart jar with a lid and discard the lemon peels. Store in the freezer.

VARIATION: For creamy limoncello, add a vanilla bean, split and scraped, to the lemon peels and vodka. At the end of 2 weeks (or 4 weeks), bring 8 cups of whole milk to a simmer with 5 cups of sugar. Simmer for 5 minutes, until the sugar has dissolved, remove from the heat, and cool completely. Add the milky syrup to the vodka and strain it into a clear bottle or jar. Store in the freezer.

lemon stick *for adults*

Part gin and tonic, part mojito, this is the lemon stick, all grown up. It packs a punch, so sip it slowly or serve over ice topped off with club soda.

MAKES 1 SERVING

Fill a cocktail shaker or a lidded glass jar with ice cubes. Add the limoncello, gin, lemon juice, and mint leaves. Shake vigorously until well chilled. Strain and serve in a martini glass garnished with a lemon twist, or in a high-ball glass filled with ice, topped up with club soda.

2 ounces Homemade Limoncello (page 100) or store-bought

2 ounces gin

1 ounce freshly squeezed lemon juice

5 large fresh peppermint leaves

Lemon twist, for garnish

Club soda or sparkling water (optional)

green-and-lemon shots

When we've got an abundance of kale in our garden, I pull the juicer out and make enough of this refreshing combination to fill two little juice glasses. It's a perfectly balanced shot of sweet-tart-spicy-green feel-good.

MAKES 2 SERVINGS

1 lemon, quartered

2 green apples, such as Newtown Pippin or Granny Smith

2 packed cups kale or spinach leaves

1-inch knob ginger, peeled

Remove any visible seeds from the lemon quarters, and cut the apples (unpeeled and uncored) into pieces that will fit through your juicer feed chute. Insert the lemon, followed by the apple and kale. Send the ginger through last and enjoy immediately.

lemon rosemary barley water

Barley water has been associated with Wimbledon for eighty years, though drinking water with boiled grain dates all the way back to ancient times. Credited with everything from nutritive to restorative properties (the Invalid Cookery section of *Mrs. Beeton's Book of Household Management* has several recipes), barley water's powers are largely unproven. As far as I can tell, its ability to refresh, whether at Wimbledon or a backyard barbecue, is reason enough to brew a batch. Use the leftover barley to make a salad.

Barley is available in hulled (still containing the germ) and pearled forms. I tried both and prefer pearl barley, which gives barley water the creamy texture and cloudy appearance for which it is known.

MAKES 2 QUARTS BARLEY WATER

In a large saucepan, combine the barley with 2 quarts cold water and half of the lemon peels. Cover and bring to a boil over high heat. Reduce the heat to a simmer and continue to cook, partially covered, for 30 minutes, or until the barley is tender but not mushy.

Meanwhile, place the remaining peels and the sugar in a large wide-mouth jar or nonreactive pitcher and, using a muddler or the back of a wooden spoon, mash the peels with the sugar to release their essential oils.

When the barley is cooked, strain the barley water into the jar and add the rosemary. Stir until the sugar dissolves, tasting occasionally to gauge the strength of the rosemary flavor. Remove the sprigs when it tastes good to you. Add the juice of 2 or more lemons and refrigerate. Leave the peels in the jar for additional flavor.

1 cup pearl barley, well rinsed

4 lemons, peel removed with a vegetable peeler, fruit juiced, divided

1 cup superfine sugar

4 sprigs fresh rosemary

staples

preserved lemons

Having tried a number of methods for preserving lemons over the years, I think I've finally landed on a favorite. The initial period of marinating in salt is transformative, removing any bitterness and replacing it with pure lemon, with a soft texture and pickled flavor. Recipes typically allow one month for this step, but I've found a week is a great start when the lemons are first cut into eighths. They continue to mellow and age in the refrigerator, where they will keep for six months or more.

You'll soon discover that preserved lemons deserve a place of honor among your favorite condiments and find yourself looking for places to include their uniquely exotic flavor. Try them in stews (Braised Beef with Preserved Lemons and Harissa, page 61), salads (Cracked Wheat and Carrot Salad with Preserved Lemon, page 20), sauces, and vinaigrettes (Summer Tomato and Green Bean Salad with Preserved Lemon Vinaigrette, page 19).

MAKES 6 PRESERVED LEMONS, CUT INTO EIGHTHS

Fill a 1-quart canning jar with boiling water. Let the water sit for 1 minute; drain the jar and invert it on a clean towel to dry. Slice off and discard the stem and blossom ends of 6 of the lemons and cut them lengthwise into eighths. Put the wedges in a nonreactive bowl. Juice the remaining lemons; you should end up with about 1 cup of juice. Set the juice aside.

1 dozen small lemons (about 3 pounds)

1 cup coarse sea salt

Extra-virgin olive oil

Add the salt to the bowl and toss the lemon sections to coat before packing them into the jar. As you fill the jar, add the salt from the bowl, evenly distributing it throughout the jar. Cover the lemons with the juice, leaving ½ inch of headroom between the juice and nonreactive lid. Let the lemons sit at room temperature for a week. Shake the jar every day to redistribute the salt and juice. After a week, add oil to cover and refrigerate for up to 6 months.

homemade ricotta cheese

True ricotta is made with leftover whey, a by-product of making hard cheese or mozzarella. Although it isn't authentic in the strict sense of the word, this simple recipe does produce a result far superior to the one sold at grocery stores. An acid—lemon juice here—is the key ingredient, separating the curds from the whey when it's stirred into hot milk. Avoid milk that is UHT—ultra-high temperature—pasteurized, a process that changes its protein structure and prevents the milk from separating. The heavy cream makes for extra-rich, silky-smooth ricotta. Though you can't make *more* ricotta from the whey produced in this recipe, you needn't discard it; it's delicious for poaching chicken or fish, making oatmeal, or using in place of water in baking recipes.

MAKES 1 GENEROUS CUP CHEESE

4 cups whole milk, not UHT pasteurized and preferably organic, such as Organic Valley

1 cup heavy cream (optional)

½ teaspoon kosher salt

3 to 4 tablespoons freshly squeezed lemon juice

In a nonreactive saucepan over medium-high heat, warm the milk, cream, and salt, stirring occasionally to prevent burning. When the milk registers 180 degrees F on an instant-read thermometer, remove the pan from the heat. Add the lemon juice (3 tablespoons for just milk; 4 tablespoons for milk and cream), stir once or twice, and let the mixture stand undisturbed while the curds and whey separate, about 15 minutes.

Line a colander or sieve with cheesecloth, unbleached paper towels, or a large coffee filter. Set it over a bowl and ladle the curds into the strainer. Let the ricotta drain to your preferred thickness; I like my ricotta to have a creamy consistency, similar to Greek yogurt. Put the ricotta in a clean container in the refrigerator and use it within 4 to 5 days.

lemon curd

I've always associated lemon curd with my great grandmother, who was Scottish. She spread it on scones, fresh from the oven, and slathered her thick buttery shortbread with it. It wasn't until I became interested in baking that I realized how versatile the yolky yellow spread is: It's a filling for cookies and tarts, or a topping for poundcake or a bowlful of berries. You can swirl it into cake batter or freeze it and serve small scoops instead of ice cream or whipped cream. Leftover curd will keep up to one week in the refrigerator and up to two months in the freezer.

MAKES ABOUT 1⅓ CUPS CURD

Prepare a water bath for the curd: Fill a medium pan with a few inches of water and bring the water to a simmer. Keep the water simmering over low heat while you cook the curd.

In a nonreactive bowl that is small enough to fit inside the pan with the water, whisk together the sugar, zest, and egg yolks. (Do this quickly: if you wait, the mixture will coagulate.) Place the bowl over the pan and whisk continuously until the sugar dissolves. Add the lemon juice and, still whisking, cook for about 5 minutes, until the mixture begins to thicken very slightly. Add the butter and salt, then switch to a spatula and stir constantly until the mixture is thick and opaque, with a consistency between yogurt and sour cream, about 10 more minutes. The curd will register approximately 170 degrees F on an instant-read thermometer.

Strain the curd through a fine-mesh sieve into a clean bowl and cover with plastic wrap, placing it directly on the surface to prevent a skin from forming. Refrigerate until firm, about 1 hour.

1 cup sugar

¼ cup coarsely chopped lemon zest (from 4 medium lemons)

6 egg yolks

½ cup freshly squeezed lemon juice (from 2 medium lemons)

6 tablespoons unsalted butter, cut into small pieces

½ teaspoon kosher salt

lemon chutney with dates and coriander

Most of the credit for this recipe goes to the late Laurie Colwin, a wonderful novelist who also wrote about food with an enthusiasm that was contagious. It is nearly impossible to read her work without wanting desperately to cook, eat, or, in my case, write about food. A lover of chutney, I went straight to the kitchen after reading her recipe and made it exactly as written. Over the years, I've adapted it, most notably by adding dates. Still, I offer it with a significant nod to Colwin.

Serve this chutney with cheese—sharp cheddar and goat cheese are good matches—roast pork, or lamb, or use it as a glaze for grilled chicken thighs. Note that the lemons need to pickle overnight, so make this recipe a day before you plan to serve it.

MAKES 2 HALF-PINT JARS

4 lemons (about 1 pound)

1 tablespoon kosher salt

⅓ cup finely chopped shallots

¼ cup freshly squeezed lemon juice (from 1 medium lemon)

¼ cup apple cider vinegar

2 teaspoons peeled and grated fresh ginger

1 tablespoon yellow mustard seeds

1 teaspoon coriander seeds, lightly toasted and crushed

Using a vegetable peeler, remove the peel from the lemons, cutting away any pith remaining on the peel. Use a sharp paring knife to remove the pith from the lemons. Finely chop the pulp and peels, discarding the seeds, and put them in a nonreactive bowl with the salt and any juices from the cutting board. Cover the bowl and let it sit overnight on the counter.

The next day, put the contents of the bowl in a nonreactive saucepan with the shallots. Stir in the lemon juice, cider vinegar, ginger, mustard and coriander seeds, pepper flakes, and brown sugar. Bring the mixture to a slow boil over medium-high heat, stirring until the sugar dissolves.

Add the dates and reduce the heat to a simmer. Continue to cook over low heat, stirring occasionally, until the mixture is thick and glossy, 45 minutes to 1 hour.

Season to taste with additional salt, if necessary. If you don't plan to use the chutney within 2 weeks, ladle it into hot, sterilized jars and process in a water bath according to the jar manufacturer's instructions. Store them in a cool, dark, dry place for up to a year.

½ teaspoon red pepper flakes

1 cup dark brown sugar

1 cup pitted, finely chopped dates (about 5½ ounces)

lemon-infused olive oil

The most common way to make infused oil is by heating it gently with the ingredient that will flavor it. But too much heat—length of time, temperature, or both—compromises the quality of your olive oil. The technique I employ in this recipe is similar to making lemon sugar, using salt instead of sugar, and a mortar and pestle, rather than my fingertips, to extract the essential oil. The result is a vibrant, lemon-flavored oil that's good on everything from scrambled eggs to roasted asparagus, in vinaigrettes and aioli, or drizzled over popcorn with sea salt and rosemary. I recommend using a good-quality olive oil for the best result. Note that the oil should infuse for three days before you can use it.

MAKES 1 CUP

2 medium lemons

1 teaspoon fine sea salt

1 cup extra-virgin olive oil

Using a vegetable peeler, remove the peel from the lemons, cutting away any pith remaining on the peel. Set the fruit aside for another use. You should have approximately ¼ cup peels. Add the peels to a large mortar or nonreactive bowl. Sprinkle the peels with the salt and, using a pestle, muddler, or the back of a wooden spoon, rub the peels with the salt until it dissolves. Add one-fourth of the oil and gently muddle the peels with the oil for 1 minute, or until the oil is very aromatic. Add the rest of the oil, stir, and cover the mortar loosely with plastic wrap. Allow the oil to infuse at room temperature for 3 days before straining it into a clean, dry glass jar. Store it in the refrigerator or a cool, dark cupboard up to 6 months.

meyer lemon–grapefruit marmalade

This gorgeous marmalade is the color of a sunset. Its flavor strikes the perfect balance of bitter, tart, and sweet, owing to the combination of citrus pulp, rind, and sugar. Making marmalade is a bit of a project, but the large yield means you have plenty for your own toast and for sharing. It will keep nicely for a year or more. Note that the uncooked marmalade needs to sit overnight, so this is a two-day process.

MAKES 6 PINT JARS

Halve the grapefruit and place them in a large nonreactive stockpot with the whole lemons. Add enough cold water to cover the fruit by a few inches and simmer, uncovered, until the fruit is very soft, about 1 hour. (Use a wooden skewer to test the fruit; it should pierce the skin easily.) If the lemons are ready before the grapefruit, remove them to a bowl to cool. When the grapefruit halves are ready, set them aside to cool.

When the fruit is cool enough to handle, hold a grapefruit half in the palm of one hand and, working over a medium bowl, use a spoon to scoop the flesh and membrane into the bowl, removing any seeds as you go. Then use the spoon to gently scrape and discard any excess pith or fibers from the shell. Halve each grapefruit shell and cut it crosswise into ¼-inch strips. Put the strips in a container with a lid and reserve in the refrigerator until the next day. (Adding the grapefruit peel partway through the process insures that it holds it shape and retains a slight chew.)

3 large red or pink grapefruit (about 3 pounds), preferably organic

4 to 6 Meyer lemons (about 1 pound), preferably organic

4 cups sugar

1 vanilla bean, split and scraped

continued

Repeat the process with the lemons, adding the membrane and any juice or pulp to the same bowl, removing the seeds as you go. Before adding the peels to the bowl, go back through and remove any seeds you might have missed. Coarsely chop the peels and add them to the bowl.

Put the contents of the bowl into the bowl of a food processor. Process until the fruit and lemon peel are finely chopped and transfer them to a copper preserving pan, or a wide, nonreactive saucepan. Add 3 cups of cold water, the sugar, and vanilla bean. Bring the mixture to a boil over high heat, stirring once or twice to combine the ingredients. Remove the pot from the heat and refrigerate it overnight, tightly covered.

The next day, add the reserved grapefruit peel to the pan with the fruit and bring the mixture to a boil, uncovered, over high heat. Cook at a lively boil for approximately 30 minutes. At first, the mixture will bubble gently. As the moisture cooks out, concentrating the sugar, it will foam. Stir every few minutes after it begins foaming. The bubbles will become small when the marmalade is close to being ready, between 222 and 225 degrees F. (Spoon a bit onto a plate and put it in the refrigerator for 3 minutes. If it thickens like jam, it's ready.) When it sets, take the pot off of the heat and remove any surface foam with a clean spoon. Remove and discard the vanilla bean. Ladle the marmalade into hot, sterilized jars and process in a water bath according to the jar manufacturer's instructions. Store the marmalade in a cool, dark, dry place for a year or more.

candied lemon ribbons

Here's a way to use zest from a recipe that calls for a large quantity of fresh lemon juice. Before juicing the fruit, remove the peel and cut it thin strips or use a vegetable peeler to remove wider pieces, which I prefer for their uneven edges and the way they curl as they simmer in the simple syrup. Garnish individual desserts with a single, sugared strip and larger items with a sparkly tangle of curls.

MAKES 20 TO 24 SUGARED PEELS

4 medium lemons, preferably organic

2 cups sugar, plus additional for coating the peels

¼ teaspoon cream of tartar, or 2 tablespoons corn syrup

Using a vegetable peeler, remove the peel from the lemons in ½- to 1-inch-wide strips, cutting away any pith remaining on the peel. Cut the peels into thinner strips, if desired, and set the fruit aside for another use.

Place the peels in a nonreactive saucepan and cover them with cold water. Bring the water to a boil over medium-high heat. Boil the peels for 1 minute, drain, and cover with fresh cold water. Repeat two more times, then drain the peels and remove them to a plate.

Using the same pan, bring 1 cup of water to a boil with the sugar and cream of tartar, stirring occasionally until the sugar dissolves. Add the peels to the syrup, reduce the heat to a simmer, and gently cook until they are translucent, about 1 hour. Allow the peels to cool completely in the syrup, then use a slotted spoon to transfer them to a wire rack set over a rimmed baking sheet. (Refrigerate the syrup for another use.) Let the peels dry for several hours, or until they are sticky, but not wet. (If they are still wet, wipe off any remaining syrup with a paper towel.) Spread a handful of sugar on a plate and toss the peels in the sugar, a few at a time, coating them completely. Store the peels in a container with a tight fitting lid for up to 3 months.

Any leftover syrup from candying the lemon peels will be thick and intensely sweet, and will keep indefinitely in the refrigerator. Use it sparingly in sweet tea, add to sparkling water to make Italian sodas, or splash it into your favorite gin or vodka cocktails. It's also good stirred into plain yogurt, drizzled over fresh fruit, or brushed on a butter and egg-rich bundt cake just out of the oven.

acknowledgments

Anyone who's written one knows that a cookbook is a collaborative effort. From start to finish—no matter its size, shape, length, or content—a book is shaped by a team, each member informing the project with a specific vision. This one began with Susan Roxborough and Sasquatch Books, who approached me last winter about writing a lemon cookbook. Thanks for the opportunity; it was a project I enjoyed enormously.

Unless the recipes are bulletproof, a cookbook is of little use. I had a crack team of recipe testers, who capably and cheerfully put my recipes through multiple tests. I'm incredibly grateful to Marianne Frisch and Sara Schrager, who together tested, documented, and offered valuable feedback on a significant chunk of the recipes. Other generous testers include Dianne and Tom McFarland, Cara Pestorius, and Jackleen de la Harpe. Thanks also to Sarah and Kevin Scaldeferri and Miriam Carson.

Special thanks to friend and ace photographer John Valls and his better half/prop stylist/project manager, Theresa Valls. I can't imagine a team better qualified to bring my recipes to life, or with whom I'd rather collaborate. Joyce Hwang's lovely design and illustrations pulled all of the elements together to create this beautiful little book.

Finally, thanks to my always supportive husband, Steven, who didn't tell me until after I'd turned in the manuscript that he might be a little bit tired of lemons.

index

NOTE: Photographs are indicated by *italics*.

conversion chart

VOLUME			LENGTH		WEIGHT	
UNITED STATES	METRIC	IMPERIAL	UNITED STATES	METRIC	AVOIRDUPOIS	METRIC
¼ tsp.	1.25 ml		⅛ in.	3 mm	¼ oz.	7 g
½ tsp.	2.5 ml		¼ in.	6 mm	½ oz.	15 g
1 tsp.	5 ml		½ in.	1.25 cm	1 oz.	30 g
½ Tbsp.	7.5 ml		1 in.	2.5 cm	2 oz.	60 g
1 Tbsp.	15 ml		1 ft.	30 cm	3 oz.	90 g
⅛ c.	30 ml	1 fl. oz.			4 oz.	115 g
¼ c.	60 ml	2 fl. oz.			5 oz.	150 g
⅓ c.	80 ml	2.5 fl. oz.			6 oz.	175 g
½ c.	125 ml	4 fl. oz.			7 oz.	200 g
1 c.	250 ml	8 fl. oz.			8 oz. (½ lb.)	225 g
2 c. (1 pt.)	500 ml	16 fl. oz.			9 oz.	250 g
1 qt.	1 l	32 fl. oz.			10 oz.	300 g

TEMPERATURE

OVEN MARK	FAHRENHEIT	CELSIUS	GAS	AVOIRDUPOIS	METRIC
				11 oz.	325 g
Very cool	250–275	130–140	½–1	12 oz.	350 g
Cool	300	150	2	13 oz.	375 g
Warm	325	165	3	14 oz.	400 g
Moderate	350	175	4	15 oz.	425 g
Moderately hot	375	190	5	16 oz. (1 lb.)	450 g
	400	200	6	1½ lb.	750 g
Hot	425	220	7	2 lb.	900 g
	450	230	8	2¼ lb.	1 kg
Very Hot	475	245	9	3 lb.	1.4 kg
				4 lb.	1.8 kg

about the author

ELLEN JACKSON trained at the New England Culinary Institute and worked for twelve years in some of Portland's best restaurants. She is presently a cookbook author, food writer and stylist, and recipe developer. She sits on the board of the Portland Farmers' Market and is a member of Slow Food Portland, Chefs Collaborative, and Portland Culinary Alliance. She is the author of *The Chefs Collaborative Cookbook*, co-author of *The Grand Central Baking Book*, and contributor to *The Paley's Place Cookbook*. Ellen lives in Portland, OR.